Implementing Intensive Interaction in Schools

Implementing Intensive Interaction in Schools

Guidance for Practitioners, Managers and Coordinators

Mary Kellett and Melanie Nind

David Fulton Publishers
London

David Fulton Publishers Ltd
The Chiswick Centre, 414 Chiswick High Road, London W4 5TF
www.fultonpublishers.co.uk

David Fulton Publishers is a division of Granada Learning Limited, part of the
Granada Media group.

First published 2003
10 9 8 7 6 5 4 3 2 1

British Library Cataloguing in Publication Data
A catalogue record for this book is available from the British Library.

ISBN 1 84312 019 4

Typeset by Servis Filmsetting Ltd, Manchester, UK
Printed and bound in Scotland by Scotprint, Haddington

Contents

PART TWO: LEARNING FROM EXPERIENCE

Acknowledgements

We are grateful to all the children and staff who participated in this study and from whom we have learned so much.

Our thanks go to Vicky Hopkins for her invaluable work on the video analysis, to Gary Thomas for his helpful guidance during the project and to numerous others who have supported us along the way. We extend our appreciation to Linda Edmans, Dorothy Morling and Seamus Feehan for their insightful comments on the draft manuscript. We also pay tribute to Dave Hewett for his commitment to Intensive Interaction and his contribution to good practice.

Finally we extend our thanks to Tony and to Lindsey for their encouragement, patience and endless cups of tea!

Glossary

accountability being answerable to others and being responsible for our actions

action research research of a social situation involving a cycle of reflection, obervation and action, carried out by those involved in the situation to both understand it and improve it

autistic spectrum disorders a collective term to include autism, the autistic spectrum, Asperger's syndrome and other pervasive developmental disorders

baseline assessment assessment of competence prior to the start of a new approach

baseline phase the period in research before a new approach (intervention) is started

contingent response an early response that links to or builds on some behavioural act of the pupil where these links are immediate and obvious to the pupil

critical enquiry research research concerned with the political and ideological contexts in which enquiry is undertaken and which seeks to expose and address inequalities

data information organised for analysis or used as the basis for a decision

developmental curriculum a term used to describe special school teaching methods and content concerned with skills and early development rather than subject knowledge

efficacy research evaluative research addressing the effectiveness of interventions

engagement a state of absorbed intellectual or emotional arousal and connectedness with another person (or an activity)

extraneous variables factors other than the 'independent variable' (the Intensive Interaction intervention) that can have an affect on outcomes and may confound (confuse) the analysis

IEP an Individual Education Plan, jointly written by teachers, parents and pupil setting out progress strategies, regularly reviewed and updated

IINCO a member of staff with a designated role for coordinating Intensive Interaction, including training and supporting colleagues

implementation the stages and process of putting something into practice

informed consent agreement given by the pupil and his/her parent/guardian to participate in something outside the normal jurisdiction of the school, such as a research project or intervention programme

innovation something new or an adaptation/imitation in a different context

inter-observer agreement meticulous use of a second person to code a percentage of the video data (usually about 10 per cent) to protect against researcher bias

interpretive research research concerned with understanding, exploring and interpreting the world, which acknowledges that there is no one objective truth

intervention phase the period in research when a new approach such as Intensive Interaction has been introduced for evaluation

intra-observer agreement meticulous re-coding of the same data over again by the same researcher (usually about 10 per cent) after at least one month duration to check reliability

lateral progression progress that is non-linear, sideways enrichment at a similar developmental level

mean the mathematical average arrived at by adding together a set of scores and dividing by the number of scores

motherese a term used to describe the talk style parents use with babies involving shorter sentences, simple vocabulary, varied pitch and lots of questions

objective assessment detached, unbiased assessment, not distorted by personal experience, feeling or knowledge

Ofsted Office for Standards in Education, the inspection board for schools

OSI (organised self-involvement) a behavioural state coded in Intensive Interaction research for when participants are preoccupied in ritualistic behaviours such as rocking or twiddling

P-levels preparatory levels that come before level 1 of the National Curriculum, introduced to aid bench-marking

peer supervision a reciprocal system of supporting colleagues by listening and engaging in joint reflection, questioning and problem-solving

PMLD profound and multiple learning difficulties, that is, profound intellectual impairment combined with physical disability or sensory impairment

positivist research research concerned with objectivity that seeks to test hypotheses, control variables, predict, measure and understand causality

PVCS Pre-Verbal Communication Schedule

QCA Qualifications and Curriculum Authority, a government body that oversees standards in training and education

qualitative methods methods that use verbal accounts and descriptions rather than numbers

quantitative methods methods that use numerical data and usually employ statistical techniques

quasi-experimental design positivist research design for testing hypotheses while recognising the naturalistic context and impossibility of controlling all variables

research ethics agreed rules and standards governing the moral conduct of research

Rett syndrome a complex neuro-developmental disorder, more common in girls than boys, featuring severe linguistic and communication difficulties that are often accompanied by dyspraxic and autistic symptoms

room management a management system that coordinates the duties and responsibilities of classroom staff in order to free up one colleague to work with an individual pupil

safeguards (or safe practice guidelines) a set of rules or procedures designed to ensure the safety and respectful treatment of vulnerable people we work with, and to protect ourselves

SATs Standardised Assessment Tasks undertaken at the end of each key stage in schools in England and Wales

SCAA Schools Curriculum and Assessment Authority, a redundant government body that oversaw curriculum assessment matters relating to schools in England and Wales

school development plan (SDP) a long-term planning tool setting out school priorities for action

session infidelity failure to conduct Intensive Interaction sessions according to acknowledged principles and practices and/or prior-agreed frequency

social physical contact physical contact of a socially communicative (non-sexual) nature such as touching someone's hand or face, hugging or kissing

stereotyped behaviours the general term for behaviours coded as OSI, which incorporates assumptions about who does the behaviours and their lack of purpose/value

subjective assessment assessment that uses rather than denies previous knowledge and feelings; assessment based on involvement rather than detachment

triangulation (also known as crystallisation) use of data from more than one source to increase the validity of findings

typical classroom activity refers to normal, everyday class activities where the pupil has access to other pupils, staff and resources

video analysis systematic analysis of video data using preordained codes of social behaviour

CHAPTER 1

Introduction

This is not the first book about Intensive Interaction, and it is not intended to take the place of other key texts that explain the approach. It is, however, the first book about Intensive Interaction written specifically for teachers, head teachers, learning support assistants and all staff working in schools. It is addressed to this audience because it is about the particular challenges of implementing the approach in schools. Our concern with some of the broader issues of assessing progress and being accountable will also make it relevant for those working in further education colleges and other educational provision.

The origins for the book are a doctoral study undertaken by Mary Kellett (Kellett 2001), supervised by Melanie Nind and Gary Thomas and funded by Oxford Brookes University. The funding was for a replication of Melanie's PhD in which she researched the effectiveness of Intensive Interaction with adult participants attending the 'school'/education centre of a long-stay hospital. We wanted to apply a similar research design to evaluate the efficacy of Intensive Interaction with children who lived at home and attended schools in the community.

In contrast to earlier evaluations of Intensive Interaction (Nind 1993; 1996; Watson and Knight 1991; Watson and Fisher 1997) the approach was relatively new to the schools and they had to get to grips with what it meant for them as a staff and an organisation, operating within a constrained context. Inevitably, the study evolved in an organic way to tell us as much about the issues of implementing the approach in schools as about the effects of using the approach for the pupil-participants. There was an overwhelming sense from the in-depth investigation that, while the use of Intensive Interaction was associated with positive outcomes for the pupils, these could have been greater if school issues were addressed. Indeed, such school issues have been little understood and under-researched prior to this study.

All researchers want their research to make a difference and we are keen that the lessons learned from this study are shared with others working in schools. We are also keen to encourage practitioners in schools to adopt their own research orientation and to find out and share more about implementation and optimum efficacy issues. We are assuming that readers of this book already have some familiarity with Intensive Interaction and some desire to see it used, or used to better effect, in their establishment. We do rehearse the key features of Intensive Interaction and outline the journey of how the approach has been implemented and evaluated across its evolution, but this is not a book about how to 'do' Intensive Interaction per se. This is already available in detail in *Access to Communication* (Nind and Hewett 1994) and in a readily accessible format in *A Practical Guide to Intensive Interaction* (Nind and Hewett 2001). *Interaction in Action* (Hewett and Nind 1998) provides reflective accounts of using the approach in a range of different contexts, including some educational ones.

The essence of this book is that we, as advocates of Intensive Interaction, must engage with the fact that practitioners in schools cannot concern themselves with approaches like Intensive Interaction in a vacuum. They operate with finite resources in largely preordained organisational structures. They are required to conform to curricular guidelines, which, in the case of the National Curriculum, can feel quite constraining. They exist within an educational marketplace whereby parents inevitably become consumers of their services, with all the implications that this entails for having something worth selling and being able to market it. And every now and again they are inspected by people with varying degrees of expertise in relation to their pupil groups and with an agenda that does not always match that of other bodies, such as the Qualifications and Curriculum Agency, who issue curricular guidelines. The context of the standards agenda means that the focus is often on the product of their efforts rather than the quality of their educational processes. Not only this, but there is a national and international drive for inclusion.

We are aware that this context is challenging. Teachers are leaving the profession and among those who stay there is considerable cynicism. They have less time to devote to reflective practice or to engage in meaningful continuing professional development. But the pupils continue to stimulate and reward. They continue to present challenges which lead to practitioners and managers grappling with major tensions, like how to address quality interactions within prescribed curricula, how to demonstrate our value of progress that is not easily recognised by all and how to make best use of the resources we have.

In this book we discuss many of the checks and balances having to be made by those doing Intensive Interaction and working in schools (and colleges) in the current era. We offer a mix of critical reflection on the issues and straightforward practical guidance. We show where we see opportunities for doing quality work and for optimising what can be achieved with Intensive Interaction in schools. All of our discussion is informed by our individual and joint research and by our ongoing communications with practitioners in the field.

The content is organised into four sections. Some of these will be more relevant for practitioners and others for managers and those with an academic interest. We hope that all are of interest, however, regardless of professional concern. In the first section, *Right from the Start*, we address the need for an informed basis for implementing Intensive Interaction in schools. Thus, we outline the key features of the approach and what is already known about its efficacy. Readers already very familiar with the approach may want to skim this chapter. We then explore some of the theory about innovation and implementation so that we have a vocabulary and some conceptual frameworks for discussing the more specific implementation issues. And we give practical guidance on putting firm foundations in place and giving serious consideration to Intensive Interaction as an important part of school practice.

In Part Two, *Learning from Experience*, we use each individual case study from the in-depth doctoral study, to inform us about implementation issues. The stories of the six individual children who took part in the study are also stories of how practice goes well and not so well. They are stories of classroom dynamics and school factors as much as stories of individual progress. While looking for patterns of communication and social development in the pupils, we learned much about the barriers and opportunities for learning in their environments. We share our lessons about emotional well-being, personal and professional support and the need for reflective practice and efficient coordination. These were real lessons learned in real classrooms with real human benefit and cost and thus we find them immensely powerful.

Part Three seeks to step back so that we can pull together some of these lessons and develop an understanding of *Best Practice* in implementing Intensive Interaction in schools. Here are some of the critical reflections and ultimately practical guidance on how we might seek and recognise optimum progress. We look at curriculum and accountability issues and share our thoughts on how these might best be addressed. And we discuss Intensive Interaction and inclusion, showing how we see this interactive pedagogy as inclusive pedagogy. This is a heavier section in that the issues we address are challenging ones and our responses reflect this and our reluctance to be drawn into simplistic or 'quick-fix' responses.

Finally, in Part Four, the *Research Frontier*, we encourage readers to engage in their own school-based research projects and provide some tools for doing this. It is practitioners working in schools on a daily basis who are doing creative, innovative, problem-solving work on implementing Intensive Interaction and other interactive approaches in challenging circumstances. There is much to be learned from these practitioners who, with or without support from mentors, and with varying degrees of resources and different levels of systematic study or formality, are finding out about what works in schools. The guidance we offer for conducting research into Intensive Interaction is deliberately pitched at readers who are relatively new to research. Other readers may also welcome the transparency this offers about our research process.

In this book we share our own findings and hope that this stimulates further finding out and dissemination, as well as more good and even better practice in Intensive Interaction. We hope that the book helps to make a difference to readers working in schools and ultimately to all those with whom they interact. We are grateful to everyone who took part in the project for their part in furthering our communal understanding.

PART ONE

Right from the Start

CHAPTER 2

Key Features of Intensive Interaction

Defining Intensive Interaction

Intensive Interaction was recently summed up as an approach 'to facilitating the development of social and communication abilities in people with severe learning difficulties (SLD) based on the model of caregiver infant interaction' (Nind and Hewett 2001: vi). This is typical of the way Intensive Interaction is defined in the literature in that it foregrounds both the aims of the approach, which focus on particular domains of learning, and the processes of teaching and learning, which are nurturing and naturalistic. The approach is also defined in relation to the community of learners for whom it is intended, that is, pupils (or anyone) with severe and complex learning difficulties who have not yet learned the fundamentals of early social communication. Included in this are pupils with profound and multiple learning difficulties (PMLD) and pupils on the autistic spectrum.

More detailed definitions of Intensive Interaction explain what actually happens when the approach is used:

> Intensive Interaction is characterised by regular, frequent interactions between the practitioner and the learner, in which there is no focus on the task or outcome, but in which the primary concern is the quality of the interaction itself.
> (Nind 1999: 97)

As we explained in the introduction, the purpose of this book is not to explain what Intensive Interaction is or how to do it. This is already done elsewhere (in *Access to Communication*, Nind and Hewett 1994, and *A Practical Guide to Intensive Interaction*, Nind and Hewett 2001). Indeed, we assume that readers will already have some familiarity with the approach from workshops or these and other texts. In pursuing our different remit of exploring how Intensive Interaction can most effectively be implemented in schools, however, we outline the key features of the approach here, together with its origins and recent developments, in order to re-familiarise the reader with what it is we are discussing.

Origins of Intensive Interaction

Intensive Interaction was developed by Nind and Hewett and colleagues at Harperbury Hospital School in the late 1980s with young adults. This was in the context of an LEA 'school'/education centre serving some of the younger residents of the long-stay institution. The historical context was a pre-National Curriculum era in which pupils with severe and complex learning difficulties had only recently been deemed educable. There was a surge in teaching methods based on a behavioural model in which curriculum experiences were broken down into small skill-based tasks that could be taught or trained incrementally and measured so that educational outcomes could be made visible. The assumption of the time was that these pupils were not capable of incidental learning.

There is notable resonance with current contexts in terms of the lack of faith in the creativity of teachers and learners, or awareness of teaching as an art rather than a science. The main difference is that in the 1980s this was seen as applicable only to the education of these pupils with special needs who were relatively new to the education system, rather than more generally applied as today.

Intensive Interaction, however, developed and became popular against a background of considerable change. Disaffection with behaviourist teaching was starting to spread (Wood and Shears 1986; Billinge 1987; Byers 1994) with growing concern that it did not promote real learning or real understanding (McConkey 1981; Smith, Moore and Phillips 1983; Collis and Lacey 1996). This was a concern in relation to the domain of social and communication development in particular. There was an acknowledgement that learners needed a *reason* to communicate in order for language to develop and that meaningful learning takes place in context. Interest in interactive approaches was growing (e.g. Smith 1987). These offered a different style and philosophy from the behaviourist model in their emphasis on learners being *active* participants – being empowered to take control of their learning wherever possible.

The teachers who developed Intensive Interaction responded to the needs they perceived their students to have and sought to address the inadequacies of the existing curriculum to meet teaching and learning priorities as they understood them. This was before teachers lost control of the curriculum or their feeling of ownership of the whole teaching and learning process. Teachers at Harperbury were able to reject other curriculum models and make use of models of learning in infancy that they saw as eminently relevant for their older learners.

Inspired and guided by Ephraim's (1979) work on 'augmented mothering', Intensive Interaction had its theoretical origins in the psychological research of the

1970s and 1980s (primarily from Britain, America, Australia and Europe) on the rich 'intuitive pedagogy' (Carlson and Bricker 1982) found within caregiver-interaction. While borrowing from the nurturing interactive style that caregivers use with infants, Intensive Interaction was never intended to 're-parent' and was distinguished from naturally occurring caregiver–infant interactions in two important regards. Firstly, the interactive games formed a core 'curriculum' of the approach and as such were constantly reflected upon, intellectualised and evaluated in a professional, pedagogical way, which enabled structure and progression to be built into the approach. Secondly, Intensive Interaction was developed in a team teaching environment as opposed to the exclusivity of the caregiver–infant relationship.

Key features of the interactive style in Intensive Interaction

Intensive Interaction was firmly rooted in key elements of caregiver–infant interaction found to be associated with optimum social and communication development (see for example, Brazelton *et al.* 1974; Schaffer 1977). These key elements are:

- the creation of mutual pleasure and interactive games, being together with the purpose of enjoying each other;
- the teacher adjusting her/his interpersonal behaviours (gaze, voice, linguistic codetalk style, body posture, facial expression) in order to become engaging and meaningful;
- interactions flowing in time with pauses, repetitions, blended rhythms; the teacher carefully scanning and making constant micro-adjustments, thus achieving optimum levels of attention and arousal;
- the use of intentionality, that is the willingness to credit the learner with thoughts, feelings and intentions, responding to behaviours as if they are initiations with communicative significance;
- the use of contingent responding, following the learner's lead and sharing control of the activity.

(Nind 1996: 50)

Mutual pleasure/interactive game

Central to Intensive Interaction is that the teacher seeks to foster interactions that are enjoyable and game-like. This directly relates to assumptions about reciprocity. Teaching/nurturing is not something that is done to pupils/infants; it is something that happens between them while they enjoy each other. The purpose of mutual pleasure as a motivator in interaction is emphasised throughout the psychological literature (Bruner 1975; Schaffer 1977; Stern 1977; Field 1979; McCollum 1984). The feedback of pleasure each interactive partner gives the other is crucial to sustaining and repeating the interactions. The pleasurable interactions then provide the perfect context for the pupil/infant to explore and discover the effects of her/his behaviour on others.

The teacher assumes responsibility for making these interactions happen, but recognises that the learner is an active, dynamic participant in them. Mutually pleasurable interactions are crucial to achieving a state of self-experience (Stern 1985). Self-experiences such as joy, fear, suspense, excitation can only be generated in a mutual interaction such as in a game of *Peekaboo* or *I'm Gonna Getcha*. As Stern (1985: 102) argues, 'these kind of experiences with another are the most totally social of our experiences, they can never occur unless elicited or maintained by the action or presence of another'. Social language and cognitive development are inextricably interwoven and the mutual pleasure of interactions play a key part in all of them (Bretherton *et al.* 1979).

Interpersonal behaviours

> Communication is achieved through the mutual modification of behaviour in response to the partner's cues.
>
> (Clark and Seifer 1983: 68)

A key feature of the nurturing interactive style characteristic of caregiver–infant interaction and Intensive Interaction is the willingness of the caregiver/teacher to adapt her/his interpersonal behaviours in response to the abilities, interests and state of alertness of the infant/pupil. Facial expressions are exaggerated to engage attention more purposefully (Stern 1974; Trevarthen 1974; Kaye and Fogel 1980). Infants also trigger much vocalising and touching (Calhoun and Rose 1988) and smiling and head-bobbing (Kaye and Fogel 1980).

Voice and language are modified such that speech is often slow, grammatically simple, high pitched or melodic in tone with frequent questions. It is playful in character and non-directive in tone. This talk style, known to support language development, has become known as 'motherese' (Weistuch and Byers-Brown 1987). Speech modifications are triggered by belief that the communication partner can reciprocate. They may, therefore, be less apparent with non-verbal pupils with complex difficulties (Nind *et al.* 2001) although much might depend on teachers' awareness of the features and power of motherese. Teachers' interactive and verbal style may also be influenced by their perceived role as a teacher, by their communication preferences as an individual, and by their intuitions (Hughes and Westgate 1997).

Timing

Schaffer (1977: 5) described caregiver-infant interactions as based 'on an elaborate interweaving of the participants' behavioural flow'. Like other researchers, he identified the importance of synchronising rhythms and timing in effective interpersonal interaction. Similarly, in Intensive Interaction, the teacher seeks to be sensitive to signals from the pupil in order to allow his/her own responses to be paced by the pupil and to make best use of the pupil's capacity for attention. The teacher is prepared to watch, wait, pause where necessary, and join in with the pupil's own rhythms in order to achieve synchronised interaction sequences. Without this sensitive awareness of the other's rhythms he/she cannot facilitate joint attention or turn-taking routines.

Alongside cueing into the pupil's temporal patterns comes cueing into signals of pleasure/displeasure/interest etc. and a willingness to make micro-adjustments in the teacher's own behaviour based on feedback. Without such micro-adjustments, often based on barely visible/audible signals of feedback, the teacher is unable to be responsive and follow the child's lead. With them, the teacher can maintain optimum states of arousal and build sensitively judged and reciprocal interactions.

Imputing intentionality

Caregivers imputing intentionality when infants are still at a pre-intentional level of communication development is understood to be fundamental to supporting infants' transition to intentional communication (Newson 1979; Trevarthen 1979; Harding 1983). Brazelton (1979: 68) describes the process in which the caregiver responds as though the infant were behaving intentionally or as though he/she were communicating. Bateson (1975) explains that by responding as if infants' behaviours have meaning, caregivers facilitate a two-way dialogue or *proto-conversation*. This is a key element in Intensive Interaction in which the teacher ascribes the pupil with sociability and meaningful and intentional behaviours. They co-construct meanings that are plausible and in some cases that are ultimately intended by the pupil. As Lock (1978) argues, it is by treating novices as social communicators that they become so.

Responding contingently

Central to the whole style of interaction is responding contingent on the behaviour of the other. A contingent response is a swift and appropriate response based upon the careful giving and receiving of signals (Carlson and Bricker 1982). The subtlety involved in contingent responding is often such that it is difficult to judge who is driving the interaction (Bromwich 1981). If contingent enough, the infant/pupil will discern that it is a direct response to her/his own behaviour (Field 1978) which will lead to a feeling that he/she can control and influence her/his environment. This sense of being in control is essential if we want the pupil to explore the environment and her/his ability to act on it. Like mutual pleasure, the feelings of effectiveness generated for both partners by contingent responsiveness also serve as a crucial motivator for further interactions (Goldberg 1977).

An important form of contingent responding characteristic of the nurturing interactive style is imitation. In the early stages of infancy, imitation of infants' behaviours by caregivers accounts for a high proportion of the interaction. Repeating back or mirroring aspects of an infant/pupil's behaviour is a way of making contingency explicit and demonstrating that they can lead and you will follow. It is a way of promoting shared attention and shared understanding (Pawlby 1977). Some imitations, especially vocalisations, can be endowed with communicative significance, and most lead to mutual pleasure (Papousek and Papousek 1977).

Being responsive in interaction is two-way – reciprocal. The responses of each interactive partner not only serve as the stimuli for the other, but also are changed as a result of the other (Bell 1968). Interactive partners signal their responsivity by activity such as smiles, coos, imitations, game playing, sustained eye contact and the adult providing a running commentary. In a world that is contingent the infant/pupil is able to detect patterns and features that are discrepant (Trevarthen 1977) as part of hypothesising and establishing inter-subjective understandings.

What Intensive Interaction aims to do

As we have outlined, Intensive Interaction is defined by its use of the interactive style usually found in parenting as we have described, but for a different purpose. Inherent to Intensive Interaction is that the style is used deliberately and purposefully to facilitate social and communication development primarily and with this emotional and cognitive development also. Nind and Hewett (1994: 10) suggest that:

> Use of interactive game becomes Intensive Interaction when we give structure and deliberate progression to the interactive processes which are not normally rationalised or intellectualised.

Unlike in the intuitive use of the interactive style in parenting, in Intensive Interaction the style is not used to promote exclusive bonds. It is, however, partly intended to foster good relationships, which are seen as essential for good teaching and learning (see Collins *et al.* 2002). Intensive Interaction has been used by parents to assist in relating, as well as fostering development (see Taylor and Taylor 1998). It is regularly used in care work to enhance the quality of lives of people with severe, complex or profound learning difficulties (see Irvine 1998; Samuel and Maggs 1998; Samuel 2001). But it was initially and remains fundamentally an educational approach.

The aims of Intensive Interaction are listed in *Access to Communication* (Nind and Hewett 1994) as follows:

• to develop sociability (including desire and ability to be with others, taking part in and initiating social interaction and understanding various ways in which social contact can be enjoyable);

- to develop fundamental communication abilities (including eye contact, facial expression, turn-taking and emotional engagement);
- to develop cognitive abilities (including social cause and effect, predicting the behaviour of others and exploring and understanding the physical and social world);
- to develop emotional well-being (including diminished fear and anxiety and knowing the joy and satisfaction of effective communication);
- to promote constructive interaction with the immediate environment;
- to promote and teach ways of spending time, other than in organised self-involvement.

Key features of the approach – how the style is utilised

In Intensive Interaction guidance on how to alter one's interactive style is in no way rigid, linear or systematic. Instead practitioners are encouraged to use a set of principles to guide their interactive processes, applying them with both intuitive judgement and careful reflection (Nind and Hewett 1994). They will employ elements from the 'idealised' list of style features that we have outlined but this will not be indiscriminate, or as if following a recipe.

The defining characteristics of Intensive Interaction go beyond the interactive style that is adopted to the role of reflection in the way that the style is used. An important factor in what makes Intensive Interaction different from the intuitive interactions of caregivers is the complementing of intuitive elements with the professional elements of planning, monitoring and critical reflection:

> Successful practitioners of Intensive Interaction manage to combine spontaneous, intuitive responding with extreme sensitivity to the idiosyncratic needs and behaviours of the individual and an intellectualisation of the developmental principles being applied.
>
> (Hewett and Nind 1998: 4)

Planning and recording mechanisms for Intensive Interaction are discussed elsewhere (Nind and Hewett 1994, 2001) and in Chapter 13 here with specific reference to the school context.

Teamwork also plays an important role in how the interactive style is utilised. Interactions between parents/caregivers and their children with learning difficulties may become more controlling and less responsive for a number of reasons. The adults may be tired or depressed. They may be anxious and therefore 'working' too hard at their interactions – driving them instead of following their child's lead. This often happens to teachers who are interacting under pressure too. For caregivers and teachers the amount of support they receive makes a difference to the quality of their interactions (Dunst and Trivette 1986). Intensive Interaction is intended to be a team approach. This allows for the all-important support, shared reflections and problem-solving that are essential for keeping the interactions going on a virtuous cycle (Nind and Hewett 1994). Teamwork also allows for continuity in approach and protects the person with learning difficulties from the possibility of being isolated from anyone who can successfully interact and relate with them.

How Intensive Interaction is developing

Since the inception of Intensive Interaction there have been developments both in the approach itself and in the wider context of research and pedagogy. Firstly, in relation to developments in the psychological research that originally underpinned Intensive Interaction, there has been some change in emphasis from laboratory-type studies to more research in context. With this trend, communication intervention approaches have become more learner-oriented with greater attention paid to the learner's social context and to pre-linguistic behaviour. The transactional nature of communication expounded in the early literature (Sameroff 1975; Bullowa 1979; Carlson and Bricker 1982) has been further endorsed (for example by Klinger and Dawson 1992; Wetherby and Prizant 1992; Nadel and Camaioni 1993; Linfoot 1994) and the relevance of previous research into early social development has been upheld.

Thus, the theoretical foundations that underpin Intensive Interaction have been shown to be still relevant. Moreover, knowledge and understanding of early communication development has been further extended. Knowledge from caregiver–infant interaction research is fuelling more studies on interactive approaches for people with learning difficulties and leading to a better understanding of the communicative behaviour of *both* parties as crucial. In Australia, Siegel-Causey and Bashinski (1997) have stressed that communication should be viewed as a triangular framework: the learner, the partner and the environmental context. Ware (1996), in the UK, has similarly done much to raise awareness about the importance of a responsive environment to facilitate effective communication. She has argued that a responsive environment is one 'in which people get responses to their actions, get the opportunity to give responses to the actions of others, and have an opportunity to take the lead in interaction' (Ware 1996: 1). The importance of responsivity in the classroom environment has been brought into sharp profile, influenced by disturbing findings of the poor quality of interactions for many pupils with PMLD (Ware 1987).

Another trend has been in the ways in which communication and communication teaching and learning are viewed. Langley and Lombardino (1987: 162) note that 'if communication is viewed as an interactive process that evolves from dynamic social interchanges in which all individuals share responsibility for the interaction, then the communication "problem" belongs to both the student and his communicative partner'. Interventions of this type might examine the circumstances when problems with social communication occur, including when impairment interferes with conscious, reliable, readable behaviours or when attention to the caregiver is too fleeting to allow them to comment and achieve joint focus.

Siegel-Causey and Wetherby (1993) have extended our knowledge base on critical aspects of pre-verbal or non-symbolic communication. They begin from the assumption that *all* individuals communicate in some way, therefore interpreting non-symbolic behaviours as potentially communicative is critical to enhancing social interaction with pupils who have severe learning disabilities. Phoebe Caldwell can be seen doing just this on her video *Learning the Language* (2002). Some of these idiosyncratic behaviours treated as communicative have been categorised as ritualistic or self-stimulatory and until recently were generally regarded as undesirable. However, researchers such as Ephraim (1989) and Murdoch (1997) and our own discussions (see Nind 2001; Nind and Kellett 2002) have challenged this judgement. Recent research has put less emphasis on stopping stereotyped behaviours and more on analysing them (Crawford *et al.* 1992) and even to using them as a basis for developing more global communication (Murdoch 1997), all of which is in keeping with Intensive Interaction.

Also recently, researchers have begun to consider the possibility that naturalistic and interactive approaches might be beneficial for children with autism (Kaufman 1994; Davies 1997; Dawson and Osterling 1997; Nind 1999; Potter and Whittaker 2001). This is in contrast to the common perception that because children with autism do not learn social competence well through natural interactions then they cannot be helped to do so (Nind and Powell 2000). Recent evaluations of the use of Intensive Interaction with individuals with autism (Knott 1998; Taylor and Taylor 1998; Nind 1999; Kellett 2000) have endorsed its beneficial effects on their sociability and communicative ability.

We turn now to developments in Intensive Interaction in the last decade. Since the exploratory beginnings of the 1980s there have been a range of evaluations of the effectiveness of Intensive Interaction. The principal efficacy studies have been Nind's (1993) doctoral evaluation of Intensive Interaction with six institutionalised adults and Kellett's (2001) doctoral study partly replicating this with six primary-aged pupils in two SLD schools and an integrated nursery in the community.

Nind's findings illustrated the developments made in sociability and communication in all the participating students. Although each one developed in individual ways, they shared some progress in common, such as looking at the teacher's face, making eye contact, exhibiting happy facial expression and making vocalisations. There was an overall increase in the time participants spent in interactive social behaviour and a significant increase in the state of being 'engaged' in interaction. All the participants registered higher scores on Kiernan and Reid's (1987) Pre-Verbal Communication Schedule and an adaptation of Brazelton's (1984) Cuddliness

Scale. Additionally the findings showed a reduction in the incidence of organised, self-involved behaviours (sometimes termed 'stereotyped behaviours').

The findings of Kellett's study reflected these earlier findings, but with a greater degree of efficacy attributed to the younger age, sometimes higher cognitive ability and less institutionalised status of the participants. This endorsement of efficacy, coupled with other positive evaluations of the approach in recent years, adds to the larger picture of efficacy that is building up. Kellett (2001) additionally found that the degree of success or failure of Intensive Interaction to facilitate development hinged around implementation factors (hence, this book). The study highlighted understandings gained about the most successful ways to implement Intensive Interaction and these are shared in the coming chapters.

We now know more about critical aspects of implementation that substantially affect outcomes, such as micro-politics, resource management, staff development, coordination and policy-making. This is significant as complacency and flawed implementation can lead to lowered levels of efficacy for Intensive Interaction. Kellett (2001: 9) observed:

> If we want Intensive Interaction to facilitate maximum benefit for maximum numbers then we have to aim for optimum implementation. This can only be achieved by systematic analysis of implementation factors which according to Gersten *et al.* (2000) is 'complex and frequently neglected by researchers'.

Kellett (2001) also concluded that an enriched quality of life for the participants was achieved, but that this is difficult to measure or quantify. Improved social interaction, wider access to group activities, a more positive attitude from staff and an increasing ability to communicate need and emotion were all evident in the data.

Other studies enrich the knowledge base surrounding Intensive Interaction. Knight and Watson (1990) and Watson and Knight (1991) evaluated Intensive Interaction teaching at Gogarburn School, looking at the interaction between six teacher–pupil dyads over nine months. The pupils ranged in age from ten to 19 years and had profound learning difficulties. Intensive Interaction sessions were videotaped on six occasions at approximately six-week intervals. The project examined whether pupils' behaviour was more advanced during Intensive Interaction sessions than in normal classroom activity, using the Pre-Verbal Communication Schedule (Kiernan and Reid 1987). The comparison highlighted several differences in behaviour, particularly in instances where the Schedule had registered a 'never' assessment. Conclusions endorsed Intensive Interaction as providing a context conducive to communication, where sociability and communicative advances were likely to occur, and members of staff could interpret and respond to them in an optimal way.

Fisher (1994; Watson and Fisher 1997) examined the progress of five pupils with profound and complex learning difficulties over a similar period, comparing

Intensive Interaction and teacher-directed group activities. Recording sheets were completed after each Intensive Interaction session and each teacher-directed group activity, and analysed together with video data. These data showed evidence of progress during both situations but it was much less obvious in the teacher-directed group activities compared to the Intensive Interaction sessions where the quality and function of behaviours was judged to be more advanced. Pupils demonstrated more enjoyment and active participation in these sessions and progressed to engaged behaviours such as eye contact, turn-taking and controlling the tempo and the direction of the interaction. Watson and Fisher (1997: 87) concluded that periods of Intensive Interaction:

> were rewarding and stimulating to both participants. The pupils showed greater levels of engagement and initiated communication more effectively than during other class activities where they played a more passive role . . . for pupils like these, often described as being totally dependent for all their needs, the importance of such experiences, which enable more meaningful involvement in their social world, cannot be overstated.

The collection of reflections in *Interaction in Action* (Hewett and Nind 1998) added narrative accounts from a range of practitioners including teachers, care staff, psychologists, therapists and parents. Smith's (1998) story of Jamie, a college student with PMLD and very challenging behaviour, describes some of the achievements from a year of Intensive Interaction, but also his regression after moving into adult residential care and losing his access to Intensive Interaction. His story illustrates the importance of continuity of approach and the need for agencies to work closely together. Stothard's (1998) account of her experience of introducing Intensive Interaction into the special school in which she worked contributes to our understanding of the impact that introducing Intensive Interaction has on staff and some of the difficulties that need to be overcome. Her findings complement the understandings of Hewett (1995) and Kellett (2001) on these issues. Samuel and Maggs (1998) and Irvine (1998) add further understanding of implementation issues in residential and day services.

The picture emerges from these small-scale, but widely contextualised evaluations that wherever Intensive Interaction has touched people's lives, positive feedback and progress in communication have been recorded. These small pockets of positive efficacy suggest that teachers should be using and evaluating Intensive Interaction. There is every indication that it makes an important contribution to the curriculum for pupils who are yet to develop early social and communication abilities, but there is also room for far greater understanding to be achieved.

Alongside the accumulation of the effectiveness of Intensive Interaction, interest in the approach has grown. Dave Hewett and Melanie Nind have facilitated introductory and continuing practice workshops in Intensive Interaction across the

UK and in Greece and New Zealand. Additionally, there is a new wave of experienced practitioners offering training and support. The approach features in the continuing professional development courses of many British universities and in training materials such as *Enhancing Quality of Life: Facilitating transitions for people with profound and complex learning difficulties* (Byers *et al.* 2002). A national Intensive Interaction conference in 2002 attracted 150 practitioners, all keen to share and learn from each other's experiences of implementing the approach in different challenging contexts.

In some ways Intensive Interaction has become mainstream. It is a coherent approach offered across specialist social services in Somerset (Irvine 1998), adult services in Oxfordshire (Samuel 2001) and school services in at least one London Borough (Nind and Cochrane 2002) as well as an approach offered more sporadically across many LEAs. It is good practice acknowledged formally by government bodies (QCA 2001a; 2001b; see Chapters 12 and 13). While the key features of Intensive Interaction are rarely actually questioned in today's climate, the current context, particularly in schools, gives rise to many questions about how to implement the approach. We hope that these are answered in the coming chapters.

CHAPTER 3

Change, Innovation and Implementation

Introduction

The focus of this book is primarily the practical aspects of implementing Intensive Interaction in schools, but it is important, nevertheless, that such practice is built on sound theoretical frameworks. The theoretical basis for Intensive Interaction is outlined elsewhere (Nind and Hewett 1994; Hewett and Nind 1998). Here we are concerned with understanding a little about implementation theory to help analyse practical situations with greater insight. The purpose of this chapter, therefore, is to distil some of the dense literature on implementation theory into what is most useful for us in our deliberations about implementing Intensive Interaction. In essence this boils down to three main concepts: **change**, **innovation** and **implementation** and to the relationship that exists between them.

One of our recurring themes is avoiding complacency and striving for optimum practice and outcomes. In order to achieve continual improvements in classroom practice we need to be reflective both about that practice and about the larger stage of educational reform. This means going beyond a focus on individual classrooms to analysing those extraneous implementation factors in the wider school that might impede or facilitate optimum progress. For many readers Intensive Interaction will be an innovative approach in school and hence a 'change' that is being introduced. Therefore we begin by looking at what constitutes 'change'.

Change

We live in a society that is in a constant state of change and we cannot escape the fact that there will always be pressure for educational change. What it is important to understand at the outset is that change is a process not an individual event. In recent decades there have been several major studies that have examined the process of change (Huberman and Miles 1984; Hall and Hord 1987; Cuban 1988; Fullan

1991). Identifying what those aspects of change should be and how to set about implementing them have also fuelled many debates about educational reform.

According to Fullan (1991) there are two critical questions to be addressed:

- who benefits from change? (the values question)
- how feasible is the approach? (the capacity for implementation question)

'Bias by neglect'

In education circles some innovations are more prized than others. These include those that are being generously funded, have government backing and are seen as likely to increase a school's performance or 'image'. One of the first things to be aware of, therefore, is the possibility that a proposed introduction of Intensive Interaction in your school may not come as high on the innovation agenda as you might wish. This is all the more reason for getting it right – for maximising impact – when an opportunity presents itself.

Implementing change

There are three possible ways to implement change in education practice:

- by using new or revised materials
- by using new teaching approaches
- by the alteration of beliefs.

Introducing Intensive Interaction in school primarily involves new teaching approaches but it may also involve altering beliefs. Much depends on the school ethos at the outset, for example, whether communication has always been considered a priority, whether reflective practice is encouraged, attitudes about teaching as an art or a science.

> In any consideration of change, it is vital to start from where teachers actually are, not from some idealised position: starting where teachers are means starting with routine, overload and limits to reform . . . for most teachers daily demands crowd out serious sustained improvements.
>
> (Fullan 1991: 118)

Change is more likely to be successful in an environment of teacher collegiality with mutual support and frequent communication.

Measurement of change

There has been much debate about measuring teacher change since Fuller (1969) first devised a developmental framework for measuring teacher concerns during a change process. The framework was known as the Concerns Based Adoption Model (CBAM) and was made up of seven stages:

- awareness
- information
- personal
- management
- consequence
- collaboration
- refocusing.

How far a teacher progresses through the seven stages is a measure of how extensively he/she adopts the proposed change. A typical scenario with regard to the introduction of Intensive Interaction might be as follows:

- A teacher becomes *aware* of Intensive Interaction through a second party.
- He/she seeks *information* about the approach by reading the literature or attending an introductory workshop.
- He/she experiences a *personal* response to this information resulting in either an internal endorsement or rejection of the approach.
- If endorsed, he/she begins the process of *managing* its incorporation into classroom practice.
- This endorsement is taken a step further when he/she begins to involve colleagues in a *collaborative* team approach.
- A final stage reflects on the whole process and *refocuses* the aims of Intensive Interaction.

At any of these stages, adoption of the change might be threatened or subverted. A teacher may not proceed beyond the second stage if useful information is not available or if the information confounds her/his own beliefs and values. The personal response may be ambivalent rather than a positive decision one way or the other. At the managing stage, if these feelings are ambivalent then he/she may not necessarily manage the approach with any enthusiasm or conviction and it may thus be doomed to fail. If the change is 'enforced' by senior management there is every likelihood that he/she will comply outwardly while inwardly subverting the process. If there are any doubts or ambiguities it is unlikely that he/she will involve other staff in any collaborative activity.

Using Fuller's model as a base, Hall *et al.* (1986) developed a means of measuring teacher concerns during implementation of new approaches via a questionnaire. This Stages of Concern Questionnaire (SOCQ) has been adopted by several researchers as a measurement tool (see Pedron and Evans 1990; Van den Berg 1993; Noad 1995). Crawford (1997) adapted the model in his study analysing teachers' journal entries. As a result of his findings, he recommended extending the SOCQ categories to take account of the complexities of implementation. He therefore suggested three additional categories:

1. Difficulty of implementation
2. Preparedness for implementation
3. Planning for implementation.

These three additional categories have particular relevance for the introduction of Intensive Interaction because they address elements that are outside the immediate control of the class teacher. The likely success of introducing Intensive Interaction is also going to depend on:

- how much opposition or support there is from senior management, governors and parents;
- how adequately trained prospective Intensive Interaction practitioners are;
- how much advance planning goes on with regard to organisation such as room management, finding appropriate places, timetabling sessions, curriculum integration and record keeping.

The literature on Intensive Interaction has always emphasised the need for preparation – but more frequently in terms of the pupil – getting to know the person through observation. When implementing Intensive Interaction as a change in school, there may also be a need for preparation in terms of staff preparedness and planning.

Innovation

Despite the common usage of the term, innovation does not need to be 'something new'. It involves changes in skills, practice and theory and can be an original creation or an adaptation/imitation in a different context. 'Any innovation in one situation may be something established elsewhere, but the implication of these assumptions is that it is a departure from what has been done before' (Hannan *et al.* 1999: 280). Thus Intensive Interaction may be a completely new initiative in your school or it may already be practised and merely awaits adoption in a different context (e.g. new class, new teacher, new pupil).

Cuban (1988) categorised innovation in terms of first and second order changes. **First order changes** are those that improve efficiency and effectiveness of what is currently being done without any substantial change to basic organisational features. **Second order changes** seek to alter the fundamental ways in which an organisation is put together. Educational innovations have more usually been first order changes and second order changes have been generally less successful.

Intensive Interaction spans both categories and, as will be shown later in the book, difficulties can arise at both first and second orders of change. It may appear easier to implement Intensive Interaction at an individual, classroom level than at a whole-school level as the latter inevitably involves second order changes. However, our experience shows that sustained success from Intensive Interaction is more likely when introduced as a second order change with fundamental alterations to the operational organisation practices in the school.

Rogers (1995) devised a five-stage model of innovation:

- Knowledge
- Persuasion
- Decision
- Implementation
- Confirmation.

Cheung (1999) considered the fourth stage of these – 'Implementation' – as particularly complex and one that required further refinement. The complexities arise from different personal and professional backgrounds of teachers; differences in the extent, scope and degree of adoption of implementation; and the unpredictability of the interactive impact of implementation on teachers. Therefore, Cheung further classified the Implementation stage into four sub-stages:

- Experiment
- Adjustment
- Mastery (we prefer the term 'Skill' to Mastery and have used this hereafter)
- Personalisation.

Putting this into the context of Intensive Interaction presents the following illustrative scenario:

- Knowledge – one or more staff learn about the principles and practices of Intensive Interaction.
- Persuasion – they try to persuade school management and colleagues of the benefits of adopting the approach.
- Decision – a decision is taken to adopt Intensive Interaction in one or more classrooms or even as a whole school.
- Implementation:
  - Experiment: staff experiment with different games and contingent interactions to get a feel for what is going to work best.
  - Adjustment: using the information from the experimental stage staff adjust their approach accordingly.
  - 'Skill': during this stage of the implementation staff become skilled in their participant interaction.
  - Personalisation: following on from the satisfaction that comes with competent skill level there is a process of personalisation where internalisation occurs and staff invest ownership in the approach and reach a value position.
- Confirmation – this stage is usually reached when there is confirmation of the

efficacy of the approach either from external assessors (e.g. Ofsted) or internal assessment (e.g. video records or developmental progress records). With evidence of its effectiveness the teaching approach is no longer viewed as experimental and is embraced into the heart of school policy and ethos.

Hannan *et al.*'s (1999) two-year research project exploring which factors stimulate innovation concluded that sources that inspired and encouraged innovation included various forms of in-service training, financial and moral support from management, previous experience of the innovation in a different context and belief in the innovation. Their research highlighted that it was easier to innovate when in a position of power and that any position of seniority renders promoting innovation easier. These are factors that will be discussed in relation to Harriet's case study in Chapter 6.

Negative innovation

Innovation is not always welcomed in educational circles. Although there are many successful innovations that improve the quality of educational provision, this is sometimes confounded by negative effects of increased workloads, undermining of confidence and competence, and inter-colleague suspicions and jealousies (Macdonald 1974). The personal costs of trying new innovations are often high. Fullan (1991) maintains that the amount of energy and time required to learn new skills or roles associated with the innovation is a useful guide to the likely magnitude of resistance. This is not a straightforward issue for Intensive Interaction as some practitioners would find a steep learning curve in adopting the approach, while for others it would be energising and have a momentum of its own.

Mamlin (1999) showed how even rational innovations may fail if they ignore the culture of the school where the implementation process is to take place. She agreed with Fullan (1991: 47) that the uniqueness of the individual setting is a critical factor, 'what works in one situation may not work in another'. Fullan also refers to two conditions where 'non-change' can occur: firstly 'false clarity' whereby individuals *think* they have changed but have only assimilated superficially; and secondly 'painful unclarity' when unclear, 'fuzzy' innovations are tried in conditions that are not supportive. False clarity has been evident in relation to Intensive Interaction when practitioners have focused on one element, such as imitation, rather than on the whole interactive style and when the reflective element is omitted.

Managing innovation

Managing innovation is highly complex and idiosyncratic and dependent on factors associated with individual teachers as well as culture (Lester and Onore 1990; Liberman 1995; Sarason 1996). Hoyle (1986) set out two basic models for managing innovation. One is through a pattern of coordination, driven from a top-to-bottom management structure; and the other is through a pattern of integration, essentially a bottom-to-top structure based on collaborative practice of teachers. Hoyle concluded that extreme forms of either model are uncongenial to teachers.

Van den Berg *et al.* (1999) also offer two perspectives on managing innovation, one a structural-functional perspective and the other cultural-individual. The structural-functional perspective views innovation as a strongly goal-directed strategy in which schools operate rationally and methodically with a systematic means of coordination steering the process. The cultural-individual perspective relies on more organic forms of cooperation and active engagement of the teachers in the innovative process. Van den Berg *et al.* state the need for a different style of innovation leadership, less directed at planning and organising and more directed at the stimulation of interaction and dynamics. They explain that 'the members of the organisation must be prepared to learn interactively and experimentally as much of the necessary knowledge and expertise is acquired on the job'. This concurs with Fullan's (1991) opinion that innovations are usually clear only after they work, not in advance. We regard introducing Intensive Interaction to a school or classroom as an innovation that benefits greatly from dynamic, collegiate experimentation alongside support from the 'top'.

Sustaining innovation

McKinney *et al.* (1999: 471) maintain that while there is an abundance of literature on concepts of change and innovation, there is very little that addresses the concept of *persistence* of change: 'It is critical that we also examine internal and external forces that sustain or hinder the change process over time.' The Efficacy-Based Change Model (EBCM) (Ohlhausen *et al.* 1992) attends to the internal processes of participants with regard to implementation of change over time, thus addressing both the common and idiosyncratic elements of change. The model is based on three concepts: concerns-based change, self-beliefs and attributional factors. The importance of the 'expressed concerns' is emphasised within the educational context (Fuller 1969; Hall 1979; Hord *et al.* 1987). These concerns exert a powerful influence on the implementation of a change and determine the kinds of support teachers find useful.

> It has become increasingly apparent as a result of studying 'failed innovations' that change must be viewed by change facilitators as a process and that they must take into consideration the needs or concerns that individual teachers express.
> (McKinney *et al.* 1999: 474)

The second concept of self-belief is explored by examining self-efficacy, outcome expectancy and outcome value. Self-efficacy is an important indicator of how much belief individual teachers have in their ability to complete a task. Outcome expectancy concerns their belief in whether success is possible in the particular context in which they are working, and outcome value refers to their belief in the importance of the innovation itself, its intrinsic worth. All three elements are necessary for an innovation to be successfully implemented. Teachers wanting to adopt an Intensive Interaction approach sometimes do not feel it can work in their context, because of constraints within the curriculum for example. It is usually belief in the power of Intensive Interaction to make a difference to pupils, based on personal experience of making this happen, that drives them/us to find solutions.

The third concept is that of attributional factors. When individuals make decisions about persisting with an innovation, they are motivated by their perceptions of the success or failure of similar past events. Weiner (1986) suggests that individuals who perceive events to be within their control are more motivated than those who perceive themselves to have no authority over events. Internal attributions reflect the perception that individual effort and/or ability are the source of success or failure, whereas external attributions reflect the perception that elements in the situation rather than within the individual are the cause of success or failure. In summary, the expressed concerns are impacted on by self-beliefs of efficacy which in turn are affected by the attributional process and these three components together contribute to the initiation, implementation and refinement stages of an innovation (McKinney *et al.* 1999).

Georgiades and Phillimore (1980) offer a set of guidelines for successful innovation. They advise that a manager of change should work with those staff who are supportive of the proposed innovation rather than against those who are resistant, and develop a 'critical mass' within the innovation project from a self-sustaining team of workers who are self-motivated and internally powered. This is what Irvine (1998) did in Somerset by recruiting volunteers from within the service to bring about a successful and sustained Intensive Interaction initiative. It is advisable to try to work change into already thriving parts of an organisation rather than where previous innovation has failed and where change is viewed negatively and to work with individuals who have the authority to carry it out.

Implementation

Implementation theory tells us that several interactive factors affect implementation. The first of these is *need*: it is important to relate need to decisions about innovation and that all those involved in the process appreciate this need. Intensive Interaction itself was developed by teachers in response to the perceived needs of their students. Second, *clarity*: everyone involved should be clear about the essential features of the innovation. Problems relating to clarity have been found in nearly all studies concerned with significant change (Huberman and Miles 1984) and can be an issue for Intensive Interaction (Nind 2000; Nind *et al.* 2001). The third interactive factor is *complexity* in terms of the difference and extent of change required.

A scale that is too overreaching and ambitious is more likely to succeed if it is broken down into smaller components that are implemented incrementally. This is not straightforward with Intensive Interaction because of its inherently holistic nature. The final interactive factor is the *quality and practicality of the programme.* Innovations being proposed need to be seen to be practical changes of quality which teachers are confident are workable. Part of the appeal of Intensive Interaction has been that it is so practical. In addition to these interactive factors teachers' individual personalities, psychological states, previous experience and stage of career all affect the implementation outcome.

Cohen (1988) refers to the importance of developing collaborative work cultures that raise morale and enthusiasm and encourage experimentation leading professionals to be more conducive to innovation. Work environments that foster collegiality, trust, support and open communication have more effective implementation outcomes. Huberman (1981) discusses the ineffectiveness of one-off pre-implementation training workshops and maintains that staff need most help *during* implementation, claiming that most forms of in-service training are not designed to provide the ongoing, interactive and cumulative learning necessary to develop new concepts, skills and behaviour. This is a crucial factor with regard to Intensive Interaction. It is important that staff obtain some support at the early stages of attempted implementation (Huberman 1981; Joyce and Showers 1988) and this was evident in the recent study where the data collector was faced with dilemmas about responding to need for support (Kellett 2001).

Fullan (1991) summarises six core themes for effective implementation outcomes:

- Leadership and vision
- Evolutionary planning
- Initiative taking and empowerment
- Staff development and assistance
- Monitoring/problem solving
- Restructuring.

Many projects that have been initially well implemented may still ultimately flounder due to lack of money, resources and staff support. Continuance depends on change being embedded into the structure in policy statements, budgets and school organisation. Successful implementation of innovations in schools also depends on extensive levels of support, from the local community, the Education Authority, head teachers and senior managers.

Evaluating implementation

One challenge for school staff implementing Intensive Interaction is to evaluate its impact. This might be in relation to the school development plan or as part of teachers' research projects for their professional and academic development. It is important in any evaluation study to understand to what extent an innovation is being implemented otherwise there is a danger of evaluating 'non-events'. For example, if a teaching approach is expected to be implemented daily and is in fact only happening once a week, researchers would essentially be evaluating a 'non-event'. Reporting implementation fidelity information, such as amount of training, length of sessions, frequency of sessions and accuracy of delivery, is crucial and yet this is an aspect of evaluation that is often overlooked. Gersten *et al.* (2000) advocate the use of fidelity checklists and state that a deeper level of understanding of implementation issues is more likely to occur when qualitative observation procedures are used combined with interviews with participating teachers.

Recent qualitative studies have used analysis of audio and videotapes to capture the nuances of implementation (see Gersten 1996; Williams and Baxter 1996) and increase our understanding of what happens in the real world context of the classroom. Some investigations of implementation are beginning to address individual teachers' understanding of the underlying thinking behind an intervention and how, and to what extent, they adapt them and whether these adaptations have integrity (see Gersten *et al.* 2000). Teachers' own modifications may result in learning outcomes that are less or more effective than the original intervention. Our investigation of teachers' understanding and use of interactive approaches (Nind 2000: 195) explored this theme of how teachers took on interactive approaches:

> Thus rather than formulaic application, one would see an interpretation of interactive approaches that allows them to fit the teacher's own practice and thinking. Rather than being problematic, this could be a healthy development, preventing the approaches from becoming static or rigid. Conversely, of course, in this interpretative process, some of the original critical thinking could be lost.

The finding was that there was indeed growth of the concept and practice, but also that some of the emphasis on process inherent in early conceptualisations of interactive approaches was being diluted.

Summary

In this chapter we have explored some of the main theories relating to change, innovation and implementation. These theories help to situate the practical guidance and illustrative case studies that follow within a theoretical framework where examples can be continually drawn upon to support points we make throughout the book.

CHAPTER 4

Firm Foundations

Introduction

Whether you are an experienced Intensive Interaction practitioner, a coordinator or senior manager it is always helpful to reflect on starting points and firm foundations. Ironically, it is sometimes our very enthusiasm that gets in the way of good practice. Keenly motivated by training workshops, some literature you have read or the progress of pupils working with colleagues, it is natural to be impatient to start. But if you take the time to lay firm foundations you will reap the benefits of more effective outcomes. We do not intend this chapter to be a 'how to do guide' – see Nind and Hewett (1994; 2001) for guidance on getting started. This chapter takes a broader view, focusing on matters of organisation, policy writing and coordination that need to be firmly in place for Intensive Interaction to operate at optimum levels in schools.

The first element we examine is ethics and what foundations need to be put in place to safeguard the interests of the pupils with whom we work. An important aspect of this is the issue of informed consent.

Informed consent

The first question to ask is do we actually need consent? This is a teaching approach after all and it is happening under the umbrella of 'curriculum'. Even though this may be true, we would recommend the seeking of consent for the following reasons:

- The emotional and often physical intimacy of the approach could place staff and pupils in vulnerable positions – gaining consent is an additional safeguard.
- Involving parents/guardians increases the chances of extending Intensive Interaction into the home environment.
- You may wish to use video cameras for record keeping, evaluation and reflection and consent is always needed for this. (If you intend to conduct a research

evaluation study then informed consent is *essential*. A more comprehensive discussion of the issues involved and guidelines on how to go about it are included in Part Four: Research Frontier.)

• The act of seeking consent is an ongoing process and therefore we constantly reflect and reappraise what we are doing with particular pupils.

In order to give consent, parents need to have sufficient information to make an *informed* choice. This accords with an ethos of maximising the sharing of information to which we would subscribe. A summary of the aims and objectives of the approach, a description of the likely content of interactive sessions and references to literature are all useful sources that give parents the opportunity to find out more information should they wish to. If you have any demonstration video of an Intensive Interaction session (with full permission for viewing for this purpose) then an invitation for parents to view this at school could also be helpful. A brief tear-off slip crumpled into the bottom of a school bag may satisfy the statutory requirements of consent, but it is not *informed* consent and while it may be legal, it falls a long way short of being ethical.

Gaining the informed consent of parents is only fulfilling part of our obligations. It is equally important to secure the informed consent of the pupil who is to participate in Intensive Interaction. You may be tempted to ask how you can do this if your pupil is pre-verbal, socially remote and seemingly unable to indicate choice. But pupils who are unable to indicate choice can generally indicate dislike or distress if we are responsive enough to pick up the signals. These signals may be obvious like crying or screaming or less obvious signs such as tension in the muscles or withdrawal.

Informed consent is not a one-off green light, rather a situation of *ongoing* consent whereby pupils and/or parents can withdraw consent at any time. Here again we are faced with the difficulties of interpreting ongoing consent for pupils with severe and complex learning disabilities. A solution we adopted for the six children who feature in the case studies in Part Two of this book was a 'circle of consent' approach (Kellett and Nind 2001). Beginning with the pupil as the central focus and surrounding her/him by trusted people who understand, care about and are able to interpret her/his distress or anxiety enables us to put in place an ongoing mechanism that safeguards the consenting status of that pupil. A typical school circle of consent might consist of teachers, carers, siblings, peer group friends and a range of support staff. All the individuals in the circle need to be aware of the Intensive Interaction approach and understand their role as sensitive interpreters of any behaviour that might signal distress, anxiety or withdrawal of consent.

This is not to suggest that the spontaneity of Intensive Interaction should be compromised in favour of 'public gallery' sessions. This would be counterproductive. But at the same time, there are inherent dangers in practising Intensive

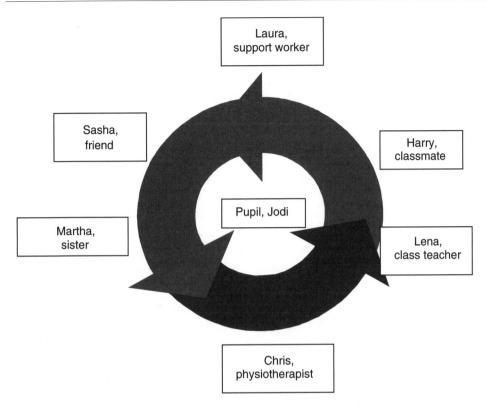

Box 4.1 Example of a 'circle of consent'

Interaction in isolation, behind closed doors. It is perfectly possible to have a productive session in a quiet area of a classroom or playground where other people can be nearby without being too intrusive.

The ethics of lone practice

Intensive Interaction works best with good teamwork. However, what happens if you do not have this option, if, for example, you are the only person interested in Intensive Interaction in your school? This can be a very difficult position and although we would not wish to deter such enthusiasm, there are some important issues to be considered with regard to lone practice and many pitfalls to avoid.

One-to-one dependency

However brilliant the interaction you individually might achieve with your pupil, you cannot be certain of securing continuity of approach for that individual. You may change jobs, move locality, become sick, be made redundant or even decide to leave the profession. As we show in Harriet and Jacob's case studies, sessions that are started and then halted can be very damaging, particularly if it is early on in the intervention and a pupil is just beginning to respond. You may have to weigh up a range of factors in order to make a kind of risk assessment. There are factors that might mean that it is worth taking the risk of starting Intensive Interaction as a lone practitioner, for example, if you can identify staff whom you think will become interested, if the pupil really is suffering from the alternative approach, if there is parental support, or if you and your pupil might get support from elsewhere.

Emotional dependency

A further consideration with regard to lone practice is the danger of a pupil becoming emotionally dependent on you. The element of mutual pleasure in the Intensive Interaction sessions may lead to a state of emotional dependence. Case study evidence reveals that Intensive Interaction sessions are often the 'high' points when pupils are at their happiest, most playful and most socially engaged. There is a danger that pupils might equate these feelings of well-being with you as a person rather than with a range of persons, with the approach or with their own actions. If this happens they may become dependent upon you for their continued emotional well-being. While you may have the very best of intentions, this kind of attachment and over-dependence can lead to distress if sessions are subsequently interrupted or terminated for any reason. We need to remember that while Intensive Interaction as curriculum seeks to foster rich teaching and learning relationships, it is not about replicating exclusive parenting-type bonds.

Professional safeguards

Lone practice of an approach that uses social intimacy can leave you professionally vulnerable. Any claims of inappropriate behaviour or professional misconduct can be difficult to defend if there are no other members of staff who understand the approach you are using. If possible ensure there is at least one other adult present when participating in Intensive Interaction. Quiet corners in classrooms or open side bays may be ideal if they provide a relatively quiet retreat from the hustle and bustle of the classroom without losing contact with the main hub. If you have to go to a separate room and there is no available member of staff to accompany you, it is wise to ensure that the door is left open at all times and that there are people nearby.

Advantages of a team approach to Intensive Interaction

Working in a team does not mean several members of staff all trying to socially interact with one pupil at the same time – quite the opposite, in fact. Intensive Interaction works on the principles of caregiver–infant interaction and therefore the one-to-one partnership is crucial. A team approach is more concerned with the overall collegiate support network. Set out below are some of the advantages that come with good teamwork. They are divided into two different scenarios, one as the only practitioner within a supportive team environment and the second where several members of a supportive team are all participating in Intensive Interaction.

Scenario 1: I'm the only Intensive Interaction practitioner, others are supportive but don't feel able to engage in the approach themselves

- Room management – even if you are the only Intensive Interaction practitioner, colleagues can support you by organising activities and groupings that free up some time for you to participate in a one-to-one Intensive Interaction session. This is particularly important in the reflection and evaluation period following the session – often a casualty of busy timetables and staff shortages.
- Soundboards – team support means there is someone there to share your Intensive Interaction experiences with – the highs, the lows and the puzzling.
- Observation – colleagues can observe some of your sessions and give you independent feedback
- Video recording – colleagues can video some of your sessions so that you can use them for your own reflection and evaluation or for record-keeping purposes.
- Infection – involving sceptical or unconfident colleagues in discussions and observations about your own practice is a good, non-threatening way to involve them. The successes and benefits of Intensive Interaction can be very infectious.
- Record keeping – a single member of staff may be engaged in the actual Intensive Interaction sessions and will record the outcomes. But other staff can be involved in recording other general progress and it is important to keep track of any occasions where sociability is transferred into other situations external to the Intensive Interaction sessions. Regular recording of general development helps to put the Intensive Interaction intervention into a larger framework where the timing of the intervention can be more easily compared to overall developmental profiles.

Scenario 2: Several members of staff are participating in Intensive Interaction

- Although one member of staff may have the lead role in the Intensive Interaction partnership, it is good to have several members of staff participating in Intensive Interaction and different personalities can elicit different responses, so you get the advantage of pooling several sets of strengths and weaknesses. It is also useful to be able to have group discussions about how each of your sessions is going and to share knowledge about what is working particularly effectively and what is not. Mutual video recording and real-time observation provides valuable team feedback.
- When several of you are participating in Intensive Interaction it is helpful to develop a common system of recording and monitoring of the session outcomes.

en several staff share the same goals and ethos it is easier to get school policy
.isions to support what you are doing in the classroom.

Communication with parents/guardians

We have already stressed the ethics of informed consent from parents/guardians. To
make the most of Intensive Interaction, however, *ongoing* communication with
parents or guardians is desirable. One way of involving parents is to invite them to
sit in on one of your Intensive Interaction sessions and then discuss it with them
afterwards. You can also comment on aspects of their interactions with their children that seem to be powerful or skilled. Encourage them to read some of the literature that has been written and/or watch any demonstration video you may have
(always ensure full permission has been granted for members of the public to view
any such material). Video footage of their own child can be particularly powerful,
but also emotional. Be careful not to make parents who have trouble playing with
their child in this way feel disempowered or lacking in skill. There is nothing mys-
terious about Intensive Interaction and this may need to be emphasised alongside a
framework for practice that parents could use.

It is helpful to be able to show parents evidence of progress, however small, so
be meticulous about record keeping. Parents may want to try some Intensive
Interaction sessions at home, alter their interactive style a little or do more of what
they already do well. It is important that they have appropriate support in this so
that they extend rather than undermine the parenting relationship they have with
their child and the work you are doing in school. Active reflection on sessions to
supplement intuitive interacting is just as important for parents as any other participant and one very likely to be overlooked.

Appropriate times and places

Is there a best time or a best place to do Intensive Interaction? The answer to this
question is far from simple. Ideally the best time for you is when you are feeling
happy, confident, enthusiastic and fresh. However, this will not necessarily coincide
with times that have been arranged specifically to facilitate an Intensive Interaction
session. You will have to make fine judgements about whether or not you think it
will be counterproductive to engage in a session when you feel exhausted or
depressed. Sam's case study (Chapter 5) illustrates what can happen in such circumstances. Your pupils may also have times when they feel tired, unwell or low,
although our experience is that the Intensive Interaction session may well 'lift' them
on these occasions. (This can happen to staff too.)

With more research we will develop a better understanding of how much
Intensive Interaction time is needed or how frequent sessions have to be to make

progress. Until we know otherwise, however, it is important that these sessions are *regular*, and preferably daily. Strict timetabling may be necessary to secure this option and requires forward planning and liaison with other staff. Hopefully you will want to participate in Intensive Interaction at opportunistic moments outside of scheduled sessions. These are very beneficial but should not be viewed as replacement sessions and they should ideally still involve some form of reflection.

Intensive Interaction Coordinator (IINCO)

Like any important area within the curriculum, Intensive Interaction requires coordination. Effective coordination enables training to be organised, resources to be secured and support to be ongoing. Valuing the coordination role enough to allocate it to a staff member as coordinator helps to ensure that Intensive Interaction does not get lost among the other competing priorities in school. In focusing in this book on school implementation issues, we are suggesting that schools serious about their Intensive Interaction work might consider having Intensive Interaction Coordinators (IINCOs). This role is being piloted in special schools that have been involved with extended action research in Intensive Interaction (Nind and Cochrane 2002).

The role of an IINCO

In this section we examine how the role of an IINCO can optimise the implementation of Intensive Interaction. Our discussion centres on eight areas:

- training
- staff relationships
- policy responsibilities
- budget responsibilities
- senior management responsibilities
- individual and whole-school monitoring and record keeping
- liaison with other agencies
- professional development.

Training

Training staff appropriately is crucial to successful implementation. At present experienced Intensive Interaction practitioners and researchers are working hard to meet the demand for initial/introductory workshops and there is an increasing need for 'advanced' workshops for experienced practitioners. Central to our thinking about Intensive Interaction Coordinators is that with this role we can create a renewable source of training personnel which can be shared within school clusters and partnerships. It is in no one's interests to have Intensive Interaction 'expertise' owned by a few. In Somerset Social Services the coordinator role has been well developed and is vital to their across-the-region coherent provision (Somerset Partnership NHS and Social Care Trust 2002).

A first step is familiarising staff with Intensive Interaction. Introductory talks in staff meetings or INSET training days are a good starting point. It might also be useful to collate a resource bank of core literature to lend to colleagues who show an interest. The second step is organising initial training workshops. 'Doing' Intensive Interaction is about operating a set of principles in a sensitive and reflective way. This means that although we can learn a lot by just observing others doing Intensive Interaction, we still need to engage with these principles to carry out the approach. If you are very familiar with the approach and the principles that underpin it then you may feel that you are able to facilitate the INSET. If you are in any doubt, however, we urge caution. In our experience, if the initial training does not adequately articulate the core principles and practices then the approach can become diluted or distorted. (Case study evidence in Part Two illustrates what happens when staff begin to deviate from these core principles and become less contingent and more directive in their style.)

Initial training is only the start. Kellett's study (2001) revealed that optimum implementation was hampered by the lack of ongoing and top-up training for participating staff. An initial training workshop – sometimes held months before staff began to use the approach – was not deemed adequate. An IINCO could bridge that gap by acting as mentor and model practitioner in such circumstances. When considering training it is also important to think about professional development. Some staff may want to pursue Intensive Interaction in formal professional/ academic development, as part of an accredited course for example, and this can feed into the culture of reflection and the practice of coordination.

To summarise, an IINCO training role might include:

- organising initial training workshops;
- arranging ongoing internal training and professional development for new and existing Intensive Interaction practitioners;
- being a sounding board, offering advice, observing sessions;
- setting up focus groups/discussion groups/support groups at lunch-time or other convenient times when staff can get together to support each other;
- liaising with other schools in the area that are practising Intensive Interaction and arranging for joint discussions to share good practice.

Staff relationships

For Intensive Interaction to work well, staff need to have good relationships with each other. An Intensive Interaction Coordinator might have an ambassadorial as well as an organisational role. It is not easy to strike the middle ground between enthusiasm for Intensive Interaction and appreciation of the doubts and scepticism that some members of staff may have. It is acknowledged that Intensive Interaction is not for everyone and that some individuals do not feel comfortable with the style of the approach. The theoretical frameworks we looked at in Chapter 3 stress the importance of innovating from a position of strength, going with the core momentum for change, not struggling with resistance. We would advise a coordinator to start with a core of committed colleagues who are enthusiastic about Intensive Interaction and support them in their practice. Reluctant staff may be persuaded to become part of the team in ways other than active practice (we have found that reluctance is sometimes due to lack of confidence rather than ideological resistance). These may include:

- cooperative teamwork to free nominated staff for one-to-one interactive time;
- operating a video camera – the safe, 'invisible' position behind a camera is a good non-threatening introduction to Intensive Interaction;
- cooperative teamwork with regard to record keeping – e.g. if eye contact is something that is beginning to emerge from Intensive Interaction sessions then it is helpful if other teachers can monitor this behaviour in other situations too;
- persuading sceptical staff not to undermine the work of practitioners, particularly in discussions with parents.

Considerable interpersonal skills are also required in supporting staff at the bottom of the 'power pyramid' when colleagues higher up the pyramid are making the practice of Intensive Interaction difficult. This sometimes happens when those with managerial responsibility for other staff, e.g. class teachers for assistants and mentors for NQTs, are impeding practice. It has also been known to happen when line managers become jealous of the success that some staff are achieving with individual pupils. As a coordinator it could be tempting to 'pull rank' here but this may not be the best solution as it may alienate the line manager even more and result in hindrance becoming subversive. It is helpful to try to depersonalise such situations so that negative feelings about the approach do not become synonymous with negative feelings about a particular practitioner. Discussions at a curriculum and policy level where the practitioner is simply a cog in this process can stress the importance of continuity from a theoretical point of view, not because the practitioner is personally angry at obstacles put in her/his way. Progress that is being made can be couched in terms of general social and cognitive development so that all staff can buy into this progress. It then becomes something that can be shared rather than something that is exclusive to the Intensive Interaction sessions (and by implication exclusive to the particular practitioners, a possible source of professional jealousy). Harriet and Shane's case studies (Chapters 6 and 10) illustrate some of the implementation difficulties associated with power pyramids and professional jealousy.

It is equally important to promote good staff relationships with senior management and governors who may be one step removed from active participation but who are pivotal players in the continued practice of Intensive Interaction in your school. Once again *sharing* success and enabling them to feel a sense of ownership in the progress that pupils are making is the key. We recommend being conscientious about providing regular written feedback reports (and if possible documentary video) and being proactive about getting Intensive Interaction on agendas and offering to do presentations to governing bodies. It is also important that statements and forecasts about Intensive Interaction appear on the school development plan (SDP).

Policy writing

Policy writing has a central part to play in firm foundations. This can be approached in three ways:

1. writing a separate policy for Intensive Interaction
2. incorporating statements about Intensive Interaction into each individual subject policy where Intensive Interaction is relevant (this is likely to be most or even all of them)
3. a combination of 1 and 2 above.

What kind of information should appear in an Intensive Interaction policy? It should include:

- a rationale for adopting Intensive Interaction. Do not be defensive – this should be a positive statement;
- the aims of the approach;
- a statement about the school's policy on touch/physical contact;
- a statement about equal opportunities (the fact that Intensive Interaction may not be seen as appropriate for all pupils or all staff is not a negation of equal opportunities);
- the place of Intensive Interaction in the overall curriculum;
- training;
- a statement about record keeping;
- a statement about how progress is assessed and evaluated.

A policy document also needs to take account of how the policy itself will be regularly reviewed and evaluated.

Reflection

In our experience reflection time is a likely casualty of busy school schedules. A coordinator could have a special responsibility to try to encourage participating staff not to omit this important element in the Intensive Interaction process. In Kellett's research (2001) there was a correlation between completing post-session reflection sheets and continued good practice, and failure to complete post-session reflection sheets and dilution/distortion of the principles of Intensive Interaction. We are not saying that it is essential to write something down after every session; thoughtful reflection is just as beneficial. What we are saying is writing something down gives a structure and a routine to the reflection process that might otherwise be glossed over or forgotten. Coordinators can encourage staff to get into good reflective habits and model this in their own practice. It might be helpful to provide staff with a *short* formatted reflection sheet for them to fill in (this must be short and useful; if it is too onerous to complete it will not be used).

Record keeping

This is an essential aspect of any coordination role. Helpful information to record might include:

- a register of pupils participating in Intensive Interaction (including start date and number of sessions);
- copies of consent forms;
- a register of staff participating in Intensive Interaction (including training profiles/updates, number of pupils they are working with and number of sessions);
- progress reports/summary reports from individual pupil/practitioner sessions (possibly from pro formas that you have provided);
- standardised assessments, e.g. Kiernan and Reid (1987) Pre-Verbal Communication Schedule;
- home report statements about Intensive Interaction progress;
- library of video data as evidence of progress;
- monitoring reports of sessions (dates, summary of content of sessions, observations and recommendations);
- whole-school monitoring/evaluation reports (e.g. mapping where Intensive Interaction is happening in the school, where it is established, where it is embryonic, where it is absent etc. – see Chapter 11);
- copies of Intensive Interaction policy documents;
- copies of any documents/reports to senior management and governors;
- coordinated whole-school monitoring system: a common system of recording progress that is easy to work with and simple for practitioners to complete so that comparisons can be made across pupils.

The checklist for coordinators below might help ensure Intensive Interaction is built on firm foundations in your school.

Coordinator checklist

- Are you keeping up to date with new literature and initiatives and do you disseminate to colleagues?
- Is there a shelf in the staffroom with Intensive Interaction literature?
- Have you started a library of documentary video?
- Are you confident that training and professional development is being properly addressed?
- Are you working proactively behind the scenes to promote good staff relationships?
- Is there a policy for Intensive Interaction which staff feel ownership of? Has it been ratified by the governing body? Have evaluation time-scales been built into the process?
- Have you taken responsibility for informed consent?
- Do you have a register of pupils and staff participating in Intensive Interaction?
- Have you set up good support group networks – reflection partners, small teams, practitioner group meetings where good practice can be shared and problems discussed in a supportive environment?
- Are you liaising with parents and governors?
- Are you liaising with other involved agencies and transfer schools?
- Have you devised a whole-school record-keeping system?
- Have you taken responsibility for that part of Ofsted preparation concerned with Intensive Interaction?
- Have you considered any financial needs associated with Intensive Interaction? Do you have responsibility for a devolved Intensive Interaction budget? Are you making the most of it? Have you got sufficient staff? Are they adequately trained? Do you have enough video cameras, Practical Guides etc.? Are your budget forecasts entered on the SDP?

Summary

This chapter has underlined the importance of continual reflection and examined some of the basics that need to be addressed early on such as communication with parents, consent issues, team building, lone practice, record keeping and policy writing so that Intensive Interaction can be firmly established 'right from the start'.

PART TWO

Learning from Experience

CHAPTER 5

Sam

Teamwork, reflective practice and emotional well-being

About Sam

Sam was five at the start of the research project and halfway through Reception Year in his community special school. Prior to this, Sam had attended a local nursery school for a year. He did not talk or sign, made no eye contact and showed no inclination to look at or towards the faces of other people. His progress records from 18 months of nursery and school chartered no significant cognitive or social development. Sam's communicative ability was at a very early pre-verbal stage and staff commented that he 'lived in a world of his own'. He had severe cognitive delay with presenting behaviours suggesting a disorder within the autistic spectrum. His general behaviour included a significant proportion of ritualistic-like *finger play*. He loved anything orange and was often preoccupied with twirling and twiddling orange objects. Sam was still in nappies and his diet was very poor because of an apparent inability to chew properly.

Intervening with Sam

Sam's teacher, Clare, was keen to try Intensive Interaction. She had attended two Intensive Interaction training courses and felt confident about using the approach. When levels of enthusiasm are high, it is tempting to just launch straight into participation. It took a lot of patience and commitment on Clare's part to refrain from doing this so that we could collect baseline data. It was vital to have a clear profile of abilities and behaviours with which to compare future progress.

In order to be able to measure the effect of Intensive Interaction with Sam we needed a very clear distinction between when the approach was and was not being used. In research terms this is measuring the effect of the 'independent variable'. The independent variable was the Intensive Interaction approach itself and all the 'extraneous variables' (e.g. other specialist approaches; change of carer; residential

Video Data

SELINE PHASE	INTERVENTION PHASE
1. 5 minutes of Sam in the classroom environment during an individual activity; staff and peers nearby for Sam to interact with them if he wished.	**1.** 5 minutes of Sam in the classroom environment during an individual activity; staff and peers nearby and opportunities for Sam to interact with them if he wished.
2. 5 minutes of Sam and Clare in a one-to-one session where Clare attempts to interact with Sam *without deliberately* using any of the principles and practices of Intensive Interaction.	**2.** 5 minutes of Sam and Clare participating in an Intensive Interaction session.

Table 5.1 Nature of the video data

placement;) needed to remain as constant as possible. Video observation data were collected in several behavioural situations but in this book we are only concerned with two: the first was during normal classroom activity and the second during a one-to-one interactive session between Clare and Sam. When the baseline phase was finished, this one-to-one session became an Intensive Interaction session (see Table 5.1). Filming was done on a weekly basis initially and then fortnightly once the project was established.

Video observation 1 – typical classroom activity

The first set of data was designed to gather information about how Sam behaved in the normal classroom environment when staff and peers were not actively interacting with him but there was plenty going on around and opportunities for him to initiate social interaction should he choose to. As far as was logistically possible, these videos were filmed on Wednesday mornings during 'choosing time' when the pupils were usually looking at picture books, doing jigsaw puzzles or playing with Lego.

Our reason for video recording Sam in typical classroom situations was that we wanted to be able to measure any progress that might spread out from the Intensive Interaction sessions into general communicative behaviour. In planning for this possibility we needed baseline data from typical classroom situations to make comparisons at a later date.

The nature of the data

So what did these data consist of and how could they be used as measuring tools to chart very small developmental steps? We devised a coding system based around

some early socially interactive behaviours so that we could measure incidence rates.
For the typical classroom environment we decided upon:

- *visual scanning* – showing interest in what is going on around;
- *head down* – showing no interest in what is going on around;
- *contingent vocalisation* – vocalising in response to a human stimulus;
- *non-contingent vocalisation* – vocalising without any apparent stimulus;
- *involvement with a toy or object* – plays with or explores a toy/object;
- *contact with staff* – initiates contact with staff;
- *contact with peers* – initiates contact with peers;
- *organised self-involvement (OSI)* – ritualistic, repetitive behaviours (sometimes termed 'stereotyped behaviours').

For the one-to-one interactive/Intensive Interaction sessions we decided upon codes of:

- *no interactive behaviours* – nothing to indicate any communicative response;
- *looking at face* – looking at or towards Clare's face;
- *contingent happy/smiling face* – a happy response to a social stimulus;
- *social physical contact* – initiates or reciprocates contact e.g. stroke/touch/hug/kiss;
- *eye contact* – eye-to-eye interaction, even of a brief nature;
- *joint focus/activity* – jointly involved with Clare in an activity or exploring a toy/object;
- *contingent vocalisation* – vocalises in response to a direct stimulus from Clare;
- *engaged* – a state of complete absorption in a shared social interaction with Clare.

The data were collected over a period of 50 weeks: 12 weeks of baseline during which we collected eight lots of data and 38 weeks of intervention (inclusive of school holidays) during which we collected 15 lots of data. To calculate incidence, each coded behaviour was scored second by second and the number of seconds expressed as a percentage of the five-minute total. For example, if 30 seconds of vocalisation were coded this would equate with 30 seconds out of a possible 300 seconds and therefore show a 10 per cent incidence.

The behaviours we coded were not all mutually exclusive; for instance eye contact might be happening simultaneously with happy/smiling face. An independent observer analysed approximately 10 per cent of the data so that we could check for any possible researcher bias. The agreement between the two sets of analysis commonly exceeded 90 per cent. The video footage yielded a mass of intricate and richly descriptive data. In addition a historical log was kept that recorded any other events in Sam's life likely to affect the pattern of his behaviour, such as illness or significant changes at home or school.

Three sets of data from the video of Sam in the classroom setting, visual scanning, playing with a toy/object and organised self-involvement, are shown here to

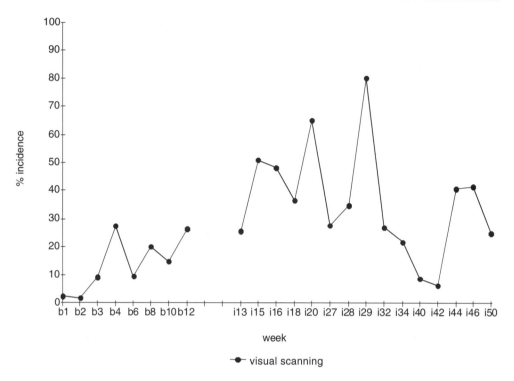

Figure 5.1 Percentage incidence of visual scanning

illustrate Sam's progress. (For a more detailed analysis of other data see Kellett 2001.) In all the tables and graphs presented in the chapters in Part Two baseline phases are indicated by the prefix 'b' and the intervention phases by the prefix 'i'.

Visual scanning was understood to involve Sam looking around him, taking an interest in his environment, rather than being completely self-absorbed. It was seen as an important precursor to social communication and had the potential effect of inviting others to approach him. Figure 5.1 illustrates what the visual scanning data showed us.

Once Intensive Interaction started the incidence of visual scanning began to rise, peaking at 80 per cent, followed by a falling trend from week 32 onwards. It might appear, therefore, that Sam made progress and then regressed. However, the data need to be analysed in terms of what *else* Sam was doing in the five minutes other than visual scanning. If the remainder of the time was dominated by preoccupation with self-involved, repetitive activity (OSI) then the reduction in visual scanning could be interpreted as regression. A useful way to track this is to view the OSI and visual scanning data together, as in Figure 5.2.

Clearly the reduction in visual scanning was not replaced by an increase in OSI; quite the reverse as the OSI reduced to a negligible amount from week 29 onwards.

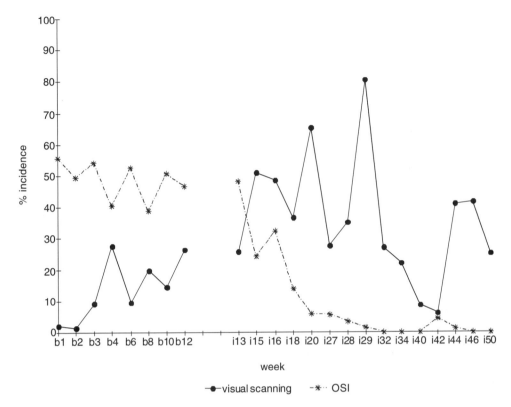

Figure 5.2 Comparison of visual scanning and OSI

In the later stages Sam began to use toys or objects in a playful way and if one also superimposes these data a much fuller picture emerges (see Figure 5.3).

From this it can be shown that once Intensive Intervention began at week 13, the OSI gradually reduced, to be replaced by visual scanning and later by purposeful involvement with a toy or object.

To demonstrate progress made in typical classroom behaviour the codes for this situation were grouped into behaviours that were 'encouraging' for others to interact with Sam and those that were 'discouraging' of interaction. A pattern of greater ability to encourage others to interact is evident after the start of the Intensive Interaction intervention. This is shown in Figure 5.4.

Summary of observation data from the typical classroom situation

In evaluating the effectiveness of Intensive Interaction, the importance of typical classroom environment data should not be underestimated because it presents the opportunity to assess whether using the Intensive Interaction approach is associated with any social and communicative progress outside of the Intensive Interaction

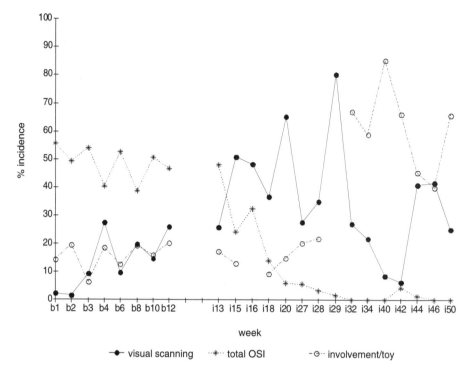

Figure 5.3 Comparison of visual scanning with OSI and involvement with a toy/object

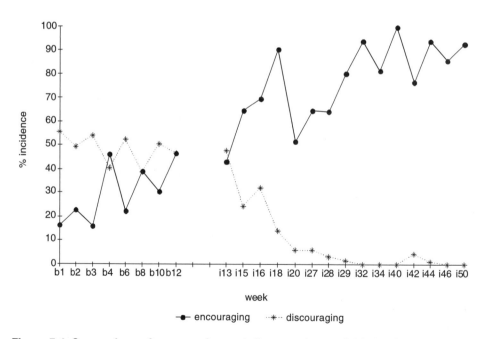

Figure 5.4 Comparison of encouraging and discouraging social behaviours

sessions themselves. The data presented here demonstrate that progress in social and communicative ability and potential approachability for others was evident in Sam's typical classroom behaviour.

'Interactive' video data

Interaction data were collected on the daily one-to-one interaction sessions (baseline phase) and Intensive Interaction sessions (intervention phase). These sessions were generally conducted in a glass-partitioned side bay used as a playroom. During the 12 weeks of baseline Clare attempted to engage Sam in social interaction without deliberately using core principles and characteristics of Intensive Interaction. At the end of baseline phase these 'interactive' sessions were replaced by Intensive Interaction sessions.

Data were collected within the normal day-to-day environment without resort to any artificially set up circumstances for video recording. This meant that on occasions pupils or teachers might be feeling unwell, stressed or depressed. In this case study, Sam's teacher Clare had a particularly traumatic personal experience. The peak of her troubles coincided with weeks 32 to 40 of the project when a shift in Clare's manner during Intensive Interaction sessions was observed and noted in the research diary as Clare became more directive and controlling.

Discussion of this observation with Clare led to her volunteering that she had been feeling depressed and drained and found it more difficult to be spontaneous and enthusiastic in the Intensive Interaction sessions with Sam. We may tentatively hypothesise about the extent Clare's emotional state affected the Intensive Interaction project. The data do not show any gross regression but one could speculate that greater progress might have been achieved during this period had circumstances been different. Certainly, from week 40 onwards when Clare's difficulties were resolved and her emotional state became more positive, there was a marked leap in Sam's progress. This situation raises some implementation issues around states of emotional well-being of staff and we explore these later in the chapter.

Sam begins to look at Clare's face

Discussions with the school staff who worked with Sam revealed that the incidence of him actually looking at or towards a person's face was virtually non-existent before the start of Intensive Interaction. We captured a 'cameo scenario' on video that illustrates the lengths Sam would sometimes go to in order to avoid looking towards Clare when she attempted to interact with him. In the toy box was a push-along train that made a whistling noise if you blew into it. Sam liked the sound of the noise but was not able to blow it for himself. He picked up the train and headed towards Clare. As he got nearer to her he stopped momentarily, turned himself through 180 degrees so that his back was now towards Clare and proceeded to walk

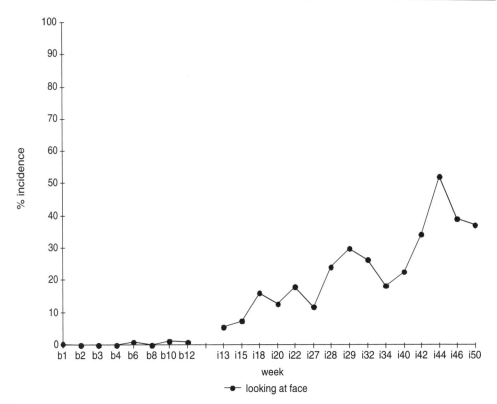

Figure 5.5 Percentage incidence for looking at face

gingerly backwards thrusting the train towards Clare as he did so. His body remained turned away from her while he waved the train in her general direction, apparently hoping that she would take it from him and blow it.

Throughout the baseline period the percentage incidence of Sam *looking at face* was negligible. Once Intensive Interaction sessions began, however, the picture changed. The incidence of *looking at face* began to emerge and reached a high point of 52 per cent at week 44. Attending to facial regard is a very important aspect of human communication (Fogel 1977; Stern 1985) and the progress made by Sam in this respect was significant (see Figure 5.5).

Sam begins to reciprocate social physical contact

During the baseline phase there was not a single incidence of Sam responding to or initiating any *social physical contact* (by this we mean using actions such as touching, stroking or hugging). Clearly it was an aspect of communication that Sam found particularly difficult and staff frequently described how Sam would repel any attempts at *social physical contact*. This also changed once Intensive Interaction had started. During playful interchanges Sam began to put his arms up to Clare to be lifted down and swung around. When Clare knelt on the floor with her arms wide

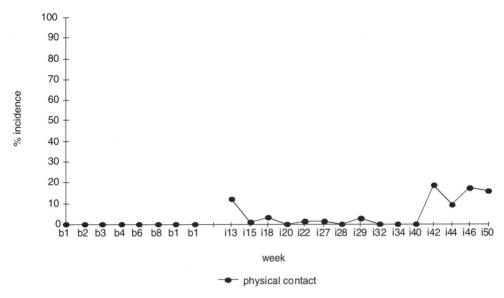

Figure 5.6 Percentage incidence of social physical contact

open he would run into them, giggling. He even began to enjoy 'dancing' with Clare, holding both of her hands and jiggling about to music. However, in the second term the progress that had been made suffered a setback. The incidence of *social physical contact* reduced considerably. This was a disappointment and it was not until a little later when Clare's personal difficulties came to light that it made any sense. Clare's depression seemed somehow to be affecting the quality of social interaction. Sam was picking up negative vibes in a similar way to a young infant responding to a mother's post-natal depression. Without realising it, Clare's playful, contingent approach had become more directive, more controlling. She was not allowing Sam to lead the interaction. Her questioning had become closed rather than open and there was less of the 'motherese' style language (Weistuch and Byers-Brown 1987) and more 'teacher talk'.

We now know that Clare's demotivated emotional state was due to a personal trauma. The graph in Figure 5.6 clearly shows a surge in the incidence of *social physical contact* from about week 42 onwards (the time when Clare's difficulties were resolved). It is tempting to speculate that greater progress might have been made at an earlier stage if Clare had been able to sustain the emotional well-being that characterised the early part of the study. Regressions of this kind concur with the literature about breakdown in interactive communication in early caregiver–infant interaction due to many causes, one of which is known to be the depressed state of the caregiver (Carlson and Bricker 1982; McCollum 1984).

A similar situation might arise in other circumstances, such as a teacher suffering from stress or fatigue or feeling physically unwell. It is interesting that all six case studies showed progress tailing off towards the ends of terms and also that surges of progress often happened near the beginnings of terms suggesting that teacher fatigue and burnout affects the quality of the Intensive Interaction. This is not surprising; we all know that our enthusiasm and teaching sparkle is not quite as good at the end of a gruelling 14-week term as it was at the beginning. That is why it is so important to engage in regular reflective practice, reviewing and analysing not just pupil progress but our own performance skills. A great way to do this is to video a session on a regular basis and scrutinise it – ideally with an Intensive Interaction buddy – for signs of staleness, fatigue, missing cues, increased directiveness and failure to make contingent responses and language/interactive style modifications. The literature on Intensive Interaction (Nind and Hewett 1994; 2001) stresses the importance of *always* taking a couple of minutes after each Intensive Interaction session to reflect quietly on two things:

1. How *you* feel about the session you have just participated in.
2. Whether anything significant happened in this particular session.

This reflection time is more likely to be skipped when we are not feeling so good, but these are times when it is particularly important. Reflection is vital to sustaining as well as improving our interaction practice.

Implementation implications

The implementation message coming through here is that Intensive Interaction works at optimum levels when staff enjoy emotional well-being. What strategies can we put in place that help to foster this frame of mind and avoid the kind of negative spiral in which Clare found herself?

A vital element in positive emotional well-being is having a strong network of support. An Intensive Interaction 'buddy' can be a great source of such support. You can invite each other to observe sessions and provide honest feedback. Most importantly, you can *share* the emotional highs and lows of progress and setbacks. Even better is a team approach where several members of staff choose to work together as an Intensive Interaction team.

In a team approach to implementing Intensive Interaction in schools there might be a lead practitioner for each identified pupil but any member of the team might interact with any of the pupils so no one need ever miss out because a particular member of staff is absent. Some staff might be better at vocal imitation than others, some more comfortable with physical interaction, and by working as a team pupils benefit from multiple strengths while still enjoying the closeness of relationship with the lead practitioner.

With a team approach it is much easier to operate room management systems that free up staff time for Intensive Interaction sessions. Furthermore, a team approach provides a degree of protection for the pupil from 'dependence attachment' whereby pupils become dependent on a lone member of staff for their social interaction. In such situations pupils can suffer grievously if the member of staff leaves the school or is absent for a long period.

Because of the attentive quality and close nature of the social interaction in Intensive Interaction staff are likely to experience more (emotional) involvement than with some other teaching approaches. This can be invigorating but it can also be draining. This is one of the reasons for keeping to short sessions and for having support networks and room management systems. You are more likely to perform at an optimum level if you can concentrate exclusively on the Intensive Interaction and not have other tensions and anxieties clouding your mind. If you are feeling low or depressed, stressed, anxious or over-tired you are unlikely to perform at your best. Wherever possible try to choose Intensive Interaction times when you are feeling good about yourself, full of energy and enthusiasm. One of the great things about Intensive Interaction is the mutual pleasure it generates for participants and if you are not enjoying the sessions then it is unlikely you will make much progress.

Other anxieties that might interfere with optimum performance arise out of the status of Intensive Interaction in your school. If you do not have the support of senior management – or class teacher if you are an assistant – and are aware there is a degree of scepticism in your school, it is going to make your task much harder. The best way to win over sceptics is with hard evidence of success. This is one of the major driving forces for this book – getting rigorous evaluation evidence out into schools where it is most needed. Sometimes senior managers are sympathetic to the ideology of Intensive Interaction but concerned about the reaction of Ofsted or governors or parents. You could ask them to read one of these case studies, or to have a discussion of the approach put onto a staff meeting agenda, or invite sceptics to come and observe one of your sessions. You can find more about implementation issues related to senior management support in Shane's case study (Chapter 10).

Sam begins to make eye contact

Eye contact was another form of social communication that was non-existent for Sam during the baseline phase. The incidence of eye contact began to emerge slowly from the start of intervention and gradually increased, commonly achieving levels above 10 per cent by the third term. Staff were genuinely surprised and delighted on witnessing something they thought would never happen, because Sam had always gone to such lengths to avert his gaze from them. Because of the zero score over the baseline phase, a strong functional relationship can be claimed between the introduction of Intensive Interaction and development of eye contact (see Figure 5.7). This kind of graphical representation is a good example of the kind of evaluation data to present to sceptical colleagues.

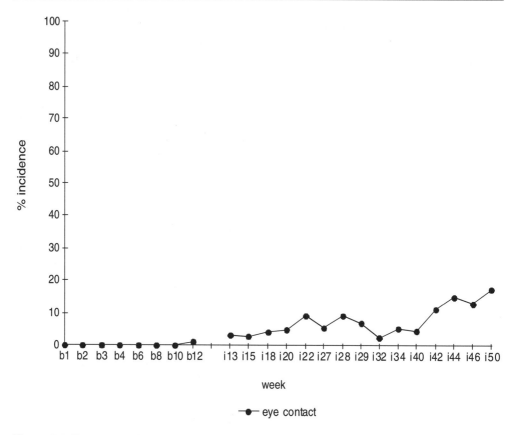

Figure 5.7 Percentage incidence of eye contact

Sam begins to enjoy sharing

The *joint focus/activity* coding category was designed to assess whether Sam was able to share a joint focus or activity with his interactive partner. Sam's progress in this area of social interaction was outstanding despite his teacher's 'depression dip' (see Figure 5.8).

Lastly, the scores for *engagement* are particularly important because they measure Sam's ability to be completely absorbed in a reciprocal social interaction and indicate progress in interactive ability. The very flat baseline – a consistent zero score – tells us that this level of interaction ability was initially far out of Sam's reach. However, once Intensive Interaction sessions started, the incidence of *engagement* began to rise quite steeply, reaching a high point of 59 per cent at week 46.

Summary of observation data from the interactive situations

The data point to a functional link between progress in sociability and communication and the intervention approach and endorse the efficacy of the Intensive

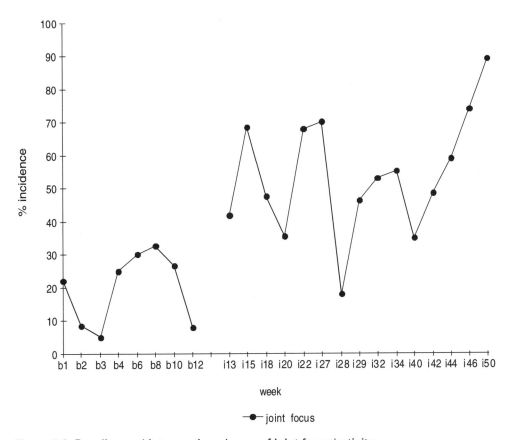

Figure 5.8 Baseline and intervention phases of joint focus/activity

Interaction approach. Also, development in social behaviours such as eye contact and *contingent vocalisation* appeared much earlier in the Intensive Interaction data than in normal classroom activity, a further indication that progress began in the Intensive Interaction sessions first, before gradually spreading into other behavioural situations.

During the baseline phase Sam spent the daily interactive sessions virtually ignoring Clare, often with his back to her, seeking out orange-coloured objects to twiddle, or racing up and down the length of the room replicating his route exactly over and over again. Towards the end of the intervention phase Sam was enjoying close social interaction with Clare with eye contact and reciprocal cuddles. He enjoyed joint activities with her, such as book sharing or dancing to music, and communicating using basic signs eventually became a regular part of this interaction.

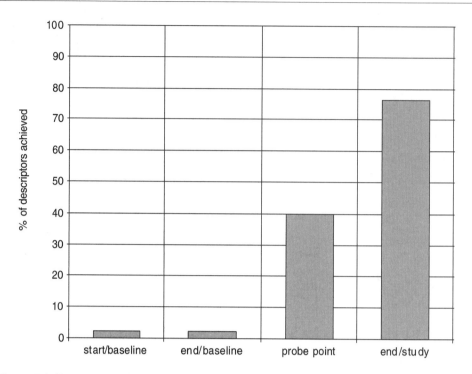

Figure 5.9 Percentage of PVCS attainments achieved at the four specified points in the study

Data from published assessment schedules

The Kiernan and Reid (1987) Pre-Verbal Communication Schedule (PVCS), a frequently used and highly respected assessment tool, was used in the research project alongside the two sets of video data. The tool provided another way of measuring progress and added to the overall richness and validity of the data. The PVCS involved judgements being made by the teachers working with Sam about his communication abilities. Assessments of each of the 175 communication descriptors were taken at four points in the study – at the beginning and end of the baseline (to give an idea of progress made without the intervention approach), then at a probe point when the intervention phase had been running for an equal time to the baseline phase, and finally at the end of the project. Negligible progress was measured in the 12 weeks of baseline compared to progress at the intervention probe point, providing further endorsement that communicative development was due to the introduction of Intensive Interaction rather than maturation or other classroom experiences.

Sam hardly figured on the schedule at the beginning and end of baseline, scoring zero in most categories. At the probe point of the study, he had attained 40 per cent of the schedule achievements and after 38 weeks of Intensive Interaction he had made quite remarkable progress, having attained 77 per cent of the entire pre-verbal communication categories. This seemed to indicate that Sam was almost ready to move on from the pre-verbal stage. This is in fact what happened and although Sam has not yet learned to communicate through speech, he has begun to communicate through sign language and by the end of the project had seven signs securely entrenched in his vocabulary. Clare informed us that Sam was signing frequently in many different situations including normal classroom activity and that this signing had been successfully transferred into his home environment.

Summary

Before the start of this project, staff described a Sam who lived in a world of his own, shut off from social interaction and unable to communicate his most basic needs and emotions. Records showed that in the 18 months of schooling, he had made no visible progress. After almost a year participating in this Intensive Interaction evaluation study, Sam had acquired seven words in his sign vocabulary, could vocally imitate a familiar tune and enjoyed mischievous social interaction with his teachers and peers. There is ample evidence that this substantial progress in his social and communicative abilities was in no small part linked to his participation in Intensive Interaction.

CHAPTER 6

Harriet

Power pyramids, session fidelity and competing priorities

About Harriet

Harriet was nine years old at the start of the project. She had severe cognitive delay and was at a pre-verbal stage of communication. She found it difficult to keep still or to focus on anything. Staff found her behaviour challenging especially as Harriet had a habit of throwing anything she picked up. Harriet did not allow anyone to get close to her or make any physical contact and there was increasing concern at her lack of progress. Harriet's class teacher, although interested in the Intensive Interaction approach, felt unable to prioritise the time needed to work with Harriet on a daily basis but Barbara, a learning support assistant who had attended the training session, volunteered to become Harriet's Intensive Interaction partner.

If staff tried to interact with Harriet she would push them away with her hands. And yet all the time she was pushing away, staff had the feeling that she really wanted physical closeness but did not know how to go about it. This was illustrated poignantly on video footage filmed during the baseline phase. Barbara was attempting to interact on a one-to-one basis (without using the principles of Intensive Interaction). Every time she tried to play with Harriet or get close to her Harriet ran away. Once at a safe distance Harriet then averted her head and body from Barbara. Close analysis of the video revealed that something else was going on. The video camera recorded Harriet with her body and head turned away from Barbara but the little finger of her left hand pointing towards Barbara in a pseudo reaching out gesture. It was as if she was saying 'I really do want to play with you but I don't know how to begin.'

Harriet had one of the shortest baselines in our study – just four weeks. This is the minimum time we would recommend if you intend to do an evaluation study. If your pupil makes good progress during a period of Intensive Interaction sessions it may prove difficult to demonstrate that this is not simply due to natural maturation unless you have baseline data of at least four weeks with which to compare it.

Obviously the longer the baseline phase or the flatter the baseline trend, the stronger your argument will be for attributing subsequent progress to the intervention. This, of course, needs to be balanced against the undesirability of withholding an approach you believe will be beneficial for too long. Optimum baseline periods for evaluation purposes are probably about six weeks or half a term and best absorbed into natural preparation time rather than being empty time.

Harriet's data (and those of the other pupils featured in this book) were collected in a similar way to Sam in Chapter 5 and we do not propose to repeat the explanatory process again here. This and subsequent case studies will simply focus on the results of the data collection rather than the process itself.

Video observation data – typical classroom behaviour

Some of the coded behaviours showed considerable fluctuation, making judgements about average incidence over the baseline period problematic. However, some clear patterns do emerge. As with Sam, one of Harriet's earliest behaviours to show an increase was 'visual scanning'. A development that occurred in Harriet's case but not in Sam's was that she began to seek out and initiate contact with staff and peers. There is video footage of Harriet walking the length of the classroom to make contact with a member of staff, actively stroking her face in a beautifully gentle social exchange demonstrating that social and communicative abilities were being transferred from Intensive Interaction sessions into more general behavioural situations.

Power pyramids

In addition to the progress noted in socially interactive behaviours, organised self-involved behaviours (OSI) were reducing. These behaviours included *teeth grinding, body jiggling* and *compulsive stroking of her hair*. The data are presented in termly blocks in Figure 6.1. The OSI, which had reduced down to negligible amounts, began to creep up again in the fourth term. This was puzzling and we set out to determine why this might be happening.

Subsequent interviews with Barbara revealed that there were two periods during the project when Intensive Interaction sessions were curtailed. This was due to a number of reasons. The first curtailment was in the second term (equates with week 15 onwards in the graphs) when Barbara was ill and away from school for several weeks. The second, a more substantial curtailment, was in the fourth term (equates with week 40 onwards) when the class teacher decided that other priorities were more important than the Intensive Interaction sessions. The project had then been running for the best part of a year. Staff shortages and projects such as the annual school production took precedence and consequently the class teacher did not

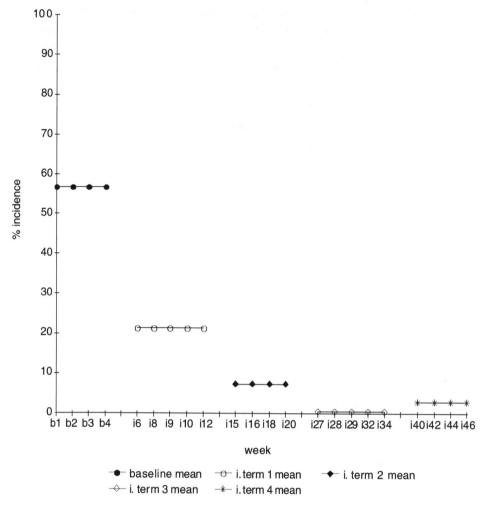

Figure 6.1 Mean values of organised self-involvement expressed in termly blocks

release Barbara to participate in many Intensive Interaction sessions. The reality was that most of Harriet's sessions in those last weeks were lost, although the true extent of this situation did not come to light until after the end of the study when in-depth interviews with participating staff took place. Barbara told us that, even though she felt strongly about the lost sessions and argued that it was affecting the good progress Harriet had been making, she was powerless to change the situation. As a learning support assistant, her relatively low status in the 'power pyramid' meant she was unable to exert sufficient influence or authority to bring about change.

It is common for assistants to participate in Intensive Interaction sessions. Indeed in some schools more support staff than teachers are Intensive Interaction practitioners. This can sometimes result in tension and less than optimum implementation because assistants do not have the same degree of power or control over resources and timetables. Harriet's experiences help us to see the importance of regular sessions and of documenting whether or not sessions are happening, otherwise any evaluation of the Intensive Interaction could be based on what Fullan (1991) calls a 'non-event'. In a climate where staff resources are scarce there is bound to be conflict between whole-class considerations and the needs of individual pupils. Intensive Interaction requires the whole focus of a member of staff for the period of the session each day plus reflection time and there will be many other important tasks competing for that time and resource. So what can we do to optimise implementation in such circumstances?

Gaining support

One of the pitfalls to avoid as a practitioner is exclusivity. The more successful and skilled you become at Intensive Interaction, the more tempting it is to feel that it is 'your baby', that you are the expert, the only person who can get these social responses from your pupil. Without realising it you may be unconsciously 'shutting out' and undermining other members of staff. Even if colleagues are not involved in the actual Intensive Interaction sessions it is worthwhile sharing your experiences with them. The more you involve them and share the thrills and spills, the highs and lows with them, the more likely they are to take an interest in the approach, value the importance of regular sessions and perhaps even begin to share ownership of the process. Even though it may seem that you are near the bottom of the power pyramid you can still exert indirect influence through your enthusiasm and willingness to share.

If tension and resistance from a class teacher are impeding progress one option is to try to get the active support of a member of the senior management team (but without undermining the class teacher). This is best done at the outset. If your school has an Intensive Interaction Coordinator, a role we argue for in this book, then you are unlikely to experience the kind of difficulties described in this chapter. Intensive Interaction will have been organised at school level so that it becomes an integral part of the curriculum. Coordinators also provide a strong advocate to turn to for help and advice. If you do not have an Intensive Interaction Coordinator you will still benefit from having an ally. Allies may be won over by evidence from the evaluations that are available; preferably share a short one as there is more chance busy people will read a brief article than a whole book. It can be helpful to highlight the most relevant sections of articles before you pass them on. Another way of gaining allies is by engaging them in conversation in the staffroom – talking about what you are doing and the effects it is having on your pupil. Enthusiasm is infectious. The more interest you can generate and the more support you can win, the easier it will be to protect sessions from the axe in times of competing priorities.

Session infidelity and competing priorities

It is difficult to determine how much progress is hindered by the loss of regular daily sessions because we are dealing with the speculative. However, one way of trying to unravel the complexities of this is to compare the mean values (mathematical average) of social behaviours term by term to see if there is any correlation between session infidelity and falling levels of progress. We look at mean values because it irons out the 'bumpiness' of the data in a naturalistic study. The individual bumps are also important and can tell us different things (such as the exact week when eye contact first began or the effect of a session when a practitioner was feeling particularly depressed or a pupil unwell), but mean values help us to eyeball the bigger picture.

It would be unethical to set out to deliberately withdraw Intensive Interaction sessions in order to assess whether progress halts or regresses without it, but when unforeseen circumstances occur that effectively mirror this, in terms of frequently lost sessions, we can learn much from such a situation. Sam's case helped to inform us about which social behaviours were first to emerge after the start of Intensive Interaction and those that took much longer to develop. In Harriet's case we are able to analyse which social behaviours were most and least vulnerable to session infidelity.

From the data we are able to show that progress in social communication begins first (and is greatest) in Intensive Interaction sessions, only later (and to a lesser extent) spreading into more general behavioural situations. Conversely when Intensive Interaction sessions are curtailed the first (and greatest) regression in social communication occurs in general behavioural situations while a critical core of social communication appears to be more robustly retained in the few remaining Intensive Interaction sessions.

Harriet begins to look at Barbara's face

The first set of scores we examine to illustrate this are those for *'looking at face'*.

The graph in Figure 6.2 shows an immediate increase in the incidence of *looking at face* once Intensive Interaction began. This progress levelled off in term two (when Barbara was ill), surged forward again in term three and levelled off again in the fourth term (when sessions were frequently lost because of competing priorities). We know from Sam's case study that *looking at face* was one of the earliest social communications to emerge from the Intensive Interaction sessions. This was also found to be so for the other children who participated in the project. With this in mind it is interesting to note that the effect of session infidelity was to halt rising incidence rather than for it to regress. This suggests that *looking at face* had become sufficiently established within Harriet's socially communicative repertoire to withstand some of the effects of lost sessions. Nevertheless, in striving for optimum outcomes, we must concern ourselves with the reality that loss of daily sessions limits overall progress.

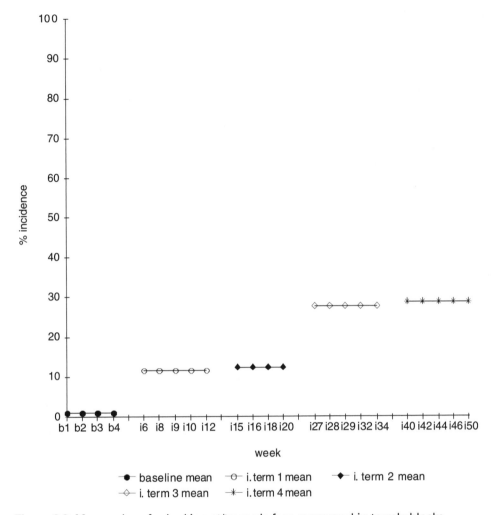

Figure 6.2 Mean values for looking at/towards face expressed in termly blocks

Emerging eye contact

A similar pattern is notable in the data for incidence of eye contact. At the outset Harriet had shown no inclination whatsoever to engage in eye contact; indeed staff commented how she would deliberately avert her gaze. Video footage and a virtual zero baseline score support this assertion. The gradual emergence of eye contact soon after the onset of Intensive Interaction was all the more meaningful because of this and Barbara spoke of how thrilled she was at this breakthrough. The graph in Figure 6.3 shows a flattening incidence of eye contact in the two identified periods when regular sessions were lost.

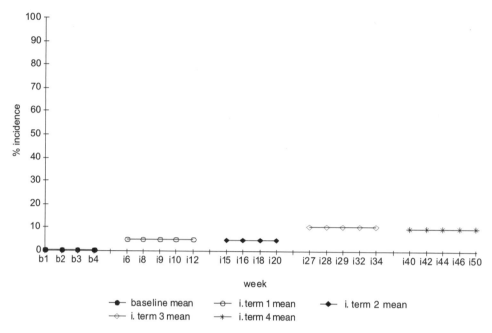

Figure 6.3 Mean values for eye contact expressed in termly blocks

Social physical contact

We now look at what we can learn from the data for incidence of *social physical contact*. This was an aspect of interaction that Harriet found especially difficult. The constant zero of the baseline indicates that making or reciprocating *social physical contact* was not a normal part of Harriet's behaviour prior to intervention. After a few weeks of Intensive Interaction this type of social behaviour did begin to emerge. The breakthrough came at week 10 (a very successful ball pool session) when Harriet fleetingly stroked Barbara's hand. Over the next weeks, incidence of *social physical contact* gradually grew (including Harriet stroking her teacher's face). It is interesting that session infidelity does not appear to have affected the incidence of *social physical contact* in the same way as *looking at face* and *eye contact*. The graph in Figure 6.4 merely shows a 'slowing' not stilling of the rising trend in the fourth term.

Video footage shows that *social physical contact* – such as touching, holding hands and stroking another's face – started in the Intensive Interaction sessions and spread into other more general behavioural situations. As Harriet began to use these kinds of social physical behaviours more widely, they became more firmly established in her communicative repertoire and as a consequence more resistant to becoming lost as sessions became less frequent. Nevertheless the 'slowing' of incidence is an issue that concerns us. Much as we applaud the progress being made, the question inev-

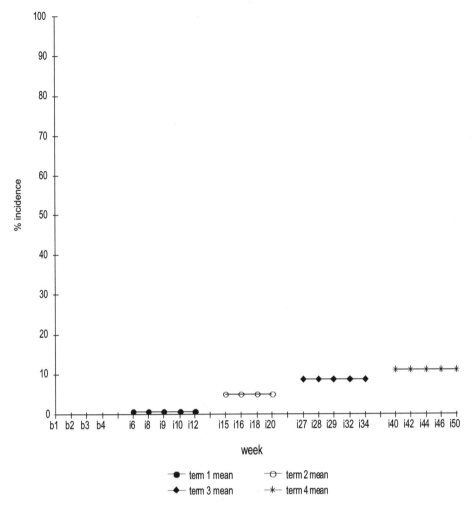

Figure 6.4 Mean values for social physical contact expressed as termly blocks

itably arises as to whether *more* progress could have been made, particularly in the fourth term when so many sessions were lost.

Attending to a joint focus

Joint focus was an interactive behaviour that developed steadily for Harriet throughout the project and does not seem to have been affected by loss of sessions. The termly mean values (see Figure 6.5) show steadily increasing incidence. *Joint focus/activity* involved Harriet sharing the experience of playing with a toy or joining in a game with her teacher and required a level of focused concentration and willingness to share body space that had been previously unknown for her. We speculate that this was a behaviour less vulnerable to session infidelity because early on in

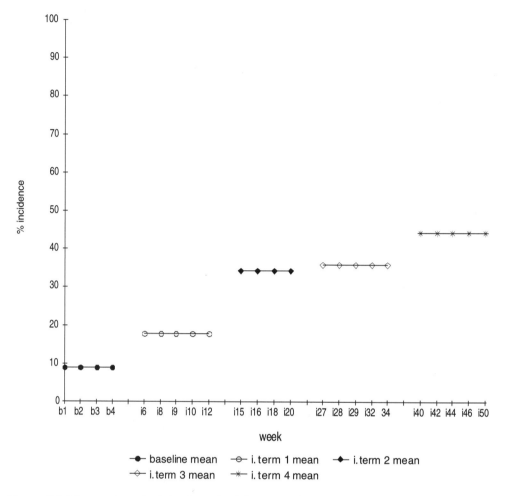

Figure 6.5 Mean values for joint focus/activity expressed in termly blocks

the study joint focus had been transferred into general classroom activity. Video footage shows Harriet 'playing' with peers and the increased incidence scores for initiating contact with staff and peers also support this assertion.

Engagement

Arguably the most crucial code defining social interaction is that of *engagement*. It can be an important indicator of the extent of social and communicative development because it requires a state of fully focused and absorbed *engagement* in a social interaction. For Harriet this was a state that became an integral part of the Intensive Interaction sessions and it was this *engagement* element that appears to have been the most seriously affected by session infidelity. Even pupils who make great progress need optimum conditions to rehearse their most advanced developments.

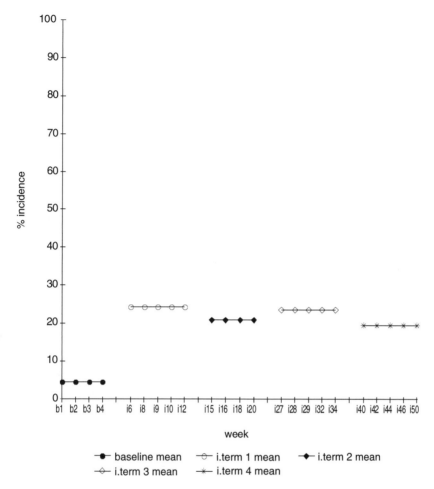

Figure 6.6 Mean values for engagement expressed in termly blocks

The graph in Figure 6.6 clearly shows two periods of regression that coincide with the periods of least frequent Intensive Interaction sessions.

The effects of session infidelity

These data highlight the difficulties associated with session infidelity and inform our understanding about optimum implementation. Optimum outcomes are more likely to be achieved with regular daily Intensive Interaction sessions. If this is not possible then it is better to at least have a substantial period of uninterrupted sessions before any reductions occur so that pupils have the opportunity to develop a 'critical mass' of socially interactive behaviours that can be successfully transferred into more general situations. Once this has happened there appears to be a degree of protection from session infidelity because the social behaviours continue to be

CONTINUES	SLOWS	HALTS	REGRESSES
Joint focus/activity	Social physical contact	Eye contact	Engagement
		Looking at face	OSI (in typical classroom situation)

Table 6.1 The effects of session infidelity on progress

practised and developed in other situations. Table 6.1 outlines the socially communicative behaviours that are most and least vulnerable to session infidelity in terms of what we have been able to infer from Harriet's case study.

This information may be helpful if you want to introduce Intensive Interaction to several pupils but only have a limited amount of staff time available. In such situations it can be difficult to decide whether to invest all of that time in one pupil so that he/she can have regular sessions each day or to spread the resources a little more thinly in order to benefit greater numbers of pupils. Obviously we would prefer a situation where adequate resources preclude such compromises but this may not be a realistic option in your school. If this is the case then our advice is not to compromise the regular daily Intensive Interaction sessions of your first pupil until you begin to observe some socially interactive behaviours emerging in situations external to the sessions.

Knowledge about the effects of session infidelity is also useful when contemplating how to manage long periods of school holidays. Awareness that loss of sessions is likely to impede progress – but less so once a certain critical point is reached – may influence decisions about when to start Intensive Interaction. Maximum 'runs' of weeks are desirable in the early stages and a starting point as far away from the long summer vacation as possible has obvious advantages. The school holidays are themselves an implementation issue and strategies regarding this are discussed in Jacob's case study in Chapter 8.

Summary of the video observation data

The video data presented here provide evidence of substantial progress made by Harriet in many important areas of sociability and communication. Particular success was noticeable with eye contact, reciprocating social physical contact and joint focus. The conditions under which the study was undertaken were not ideal with many obstacles such as loss of sessions, staff shortages and difficulties sur-

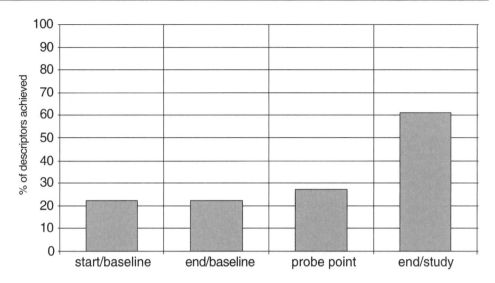

Figure 6.7 Percentage of PVCS attainments achieved at the four specified points in the study

rounding the power to effect change and prioritise resources ultimately getting in the way of optimum progress. However, while seeking to understand what conditions foster optimum outcomes, we do not wish to dwell unduly on the negatives. There is much to celebrate in Harriet's case study and the next section addresses this by examining the progress that was measured through published assessment schedules. One of these was the Kiernan and Reid (1987) Pre-Verbal Communication Schedule. Measurements were taken at four points in the study (as described in Sam's case study).

The raw scores from each of the 175 behaviour descriptors have been converted to percentages and are illustrated in Figure 6.7. The overall increase in Harriet's achievements on the Pre-Verbal Schedule rises from 22 per cent at the beginning of the project to 61 per cent by the end of the study.

Summary

Before Intensive Interaction, Harriet's school day consisted of very little social interaction. She made no eye contact and would avert her gaze from the general direction of another's face. Her typical classroom behaviour was characterised by running away from social physical contact. The throwing gesture, which was prevalent enough to be scored separately as an idiosyncratic code, was also present in the way Harriet coped with this. There is frequent video evidence and noted staff comments of Harriet pushing away with a kind of 'throwing action' the hands and bodies of peers or staff who tried to engage her in social interaction. By the end of the study she was participating in warm, affectionate interactions with staff in the classroom environment. Staff commented on how persistent Harriet had become in seeking out staff in order to interact with them, grabbing their hands, clapping in their faces and making deliberate eye contact so that they could not ignore her.

These are exciting developments and can be shown to be functionally linked to the introduction of the Intensive Interaction approach (see Kellett 2001). But while celebrating this progress we remind ourselves of the greater progress that might have been made if issues such as of session fidelity, competing priorities and power pyramids had not had a part to play.

CHAPTER 7

Catherine

Quality of life in death

Introduction

Catherine, our next participant in the Kellett (2001) evaluation study, died part-way through that project. Although Catherine's data-set is incomplete there is much we can learn from her case study about the relevance of Intensive Interaction for children with very profound and complex learning difficulties and those who may also have shortened life expectancies. Most of all Catherine's story raises important issues about quality of life.

About Catherine

Catherine was 11 years old at the beginning of the study. She had profound learning and communication difficulties compounded by quadriplegia, visual impairment, poor hearing and seizures. She had severe and frequent muscle spasms and her joints were prone to dislocation problems. Catherine was unable to eat normally and relied on a gastrostomy feeding tube. Her multiple impairments rendered her very frail and particularly vulnerable to catching infections and illnesses.

Catherine lived at home with her parents and younger sibling but spent one in three weekends and occasional nights in respite care at a local hospice. She attended a community special school where she was taught in an upper junior class. It had been established that Catherine had a small amount of sight in one eye and reasonable hearing but her mobility was restricted to a few small movements of the head and part of one hand. She produced no sounds or vocalisations. Staff had learned to interpret distress from facial expressions such as screwing her chin.

Catherine was chosen for the study in consultation with the head teacher and staff who felt that any development in social communication, however small, would improve the quality of her life. Catherine's participation in the project was met with enthusiasm by her parents who were equally committed to any intervention that might develop her social communication and improve the quality of her life. The class teacher, Liz, volunteered to be Catherine's Intensive Interaction partner.

Scrutiny of school records and discussions with staff revealed that Catherine had made negligible progress in the previous few years. Staff regarded her as a passive pupil who made no eye contact, no vocalisations of any kind and whose visual scanning was scant. The pervasive impression was that things were done *to* Catherine rather than *with* her; she was fed, she was dressed, she was cared for, she was talked to, but staff did not feel that there was any participation or interaction on these occasions.

Because of the severity of her impairments and the absence of any progress it was intended that Catherine would have a short baseline phase of four weeks. Unfortunately she was too poorly to attend school in weeks 4 and 5 and this disruption meant that the baseline phase had to be re-established and thus ended up as six measurement points recorded on weeks 1, 2, 3, 6, 7 and 8. Additional periods of illness and a week away on a residential trip further disrupted the symmetry of the research design. From the two terms that Catherine participated in the project only six baseline and five Intensive Interaction data points were able to be collected. A degree of caution is therefore required and the data provide more of a 'descriptive snapshot' than an empirical evaluation. However, the value of Catherine's story should not be underestimated. It provides us with some richly descriptive data which, although incomplete, nevertheless add to the cumulative bank of knowledge amassed from the project as a whole. Our experiences with Catherine affirm the positive message about not allowing the severity of impairment to deter us from trying Intensive Interaction and that it is never too late to start – even if a child has a limited life expectancy. When we took the decision to include Catherine in the project it was with the full knowledge that her extreme frailty meant that her death was a very real possibility.

Because of the small amount of data on Catherine we have decided to include additional data from the Kellett (2001) study: two other behavioural situations. These were part of a Sociability Observation Schedule (Nind 1996) concerned with measuring responses that encourage (or not) interaction. These data were collected on the same weeks as the main data and help to fill out the picture. The first of these are three-minute video observations of Catherine when Liz was sitting in close proximity to her but not seeking to engage her in social interaction. The second are three-minute video observations when Liz attempted to engage Catherine in social interaction solely by using *social physical contact*. This took the form of Liz stroking and patting Catherine's face and her one good hand. But first we examine the data from the video observations of typical classroom behaviour.

	makes contact with staff	makes contact with peer	visual scanning	OSI	sleeping /eyes closed	head down	non-contingent vocalising	contingent vocalising	purposeful involvement with toy/object	passive stare	screwing chin
b1	0	0	8	0	6	0	0	0	0	86	5.3
b2	0	0	13.7	0	0	0	0	0	0	86.9	3.7
b3	0	0	18.6	0	67.6	0	0	0	0	13.6	0
b6	0	0	47.3	0	0	0	0	0	0	52.7	2.7
b7	0	0	21.3	0	78.7	0	0	0	0	0	0
b8*	0	0	13.7	0	62.7	0	0	0	0	23.7	0
i10	0	0	74.3	0	0	0	0	0	0	25.7	4.7
i12	0	8	26	0	58.7	0	0	0	0	15.3	0
i13	0	0	37.7	0	0	0	0	0	0	54.3	3.3
i14	0	0	22.3	0	0	0	0	0	0	77.7	4
i16*	0	0	0	0	100	0	0	0	0	0	0

* semi-sedated

Table 7.1 Percentage incidence of behaviours in typical classroom observations

Video observation data – typical classroom behaviour

These video observations were designed to gather data about how Catherine behaved when staff and peers were not actively interacting with her, although there was always plenty of activity going on around her should Catherine choose to become involved. Catherine was always in her wheelchair for these sessions. The same common codes were used, as detailed in Sam's case study. Two idiosyncratic codes were added for Catherine which were categorised as *fixed/passive stare* and *screwing her chin.* The first code was needed because Catherine only had movement in her head and neck. Any interaction was therefore centred in the area of the head and thus a fixed/passive stare was interpreted as a negative interactive state. The second code of Catherine screwing her chin was understood by her carers to be an expression of discomfort or distress.

As has been shown with the other participants, the most rapid progress in sociability and communication occurs in the Intensive Interaction sessions and it takes longer for the benefits to filter through into typical classroom behaviour. Given that Catherine had such a relatively short amount of Intensive Interaction time we were not expecting to see any evidence of developing social behaviour transferring into general behaviour. The behaviour incidence scores in Table 7.1 seem to support this hypothesis with one notable exception – visual scanning. There was an increase in visual scanning from a mean of 20 per cent in the baseline phase to a mean of 32 per cent in the intervention phase. If week 16 (when Catherine was in a state of semi-sedation and spent all of the measured time with her eyes closed) is excluded from this analysis then the mean value is even higher, 40 per cent. Reflecting back on Sam's and Harriet's case studies and forward to the other three case studies, we notice that visual scanning was the first social behaviour to emerge. It would appear therefore that some social development was already beginning for Catherine and her death prevented us from knowing whether this might have developed further as happened with other pupils in the study. Although we do not have strong data to support a hypothesis that Catherine would have continued to develop socially, we do have a lot of strong data for the other five pupils and this close association considerably strengthens such a hypothesis.

Close proximity

Close proximity was one of the measures from the Sociability Observation Schedule referred to earlier. It was a shorter video observation – three minutes – and was designed to assess whether the *close proximity* of Catherine's interactive partner prompted any attempt at social communication. Codes such as turning her head towards Liz or making a happy face were interpreted as encouraging signs of this, whereas turning her head away or screwing her chin were interpreted as discouraging signs. Liz positioned herself slightly to the side of Catherine's wheelchair so that Catherine would have to make a deliberate effort if she wanted to turn her head towards Liz. Such an action took a great deal of physical effort on Catherine's part and was seen by staff as an important and deliberate social act. The graph in Figure 7.1 shows a noticeable increase in the amount of time Catherine spent with her head turned towards Liz.

Social physical contact

There is some interesting data from the second Sociability Observation Schedule measure. In this, teacher Liz attempted to interact with Catherine using *social physical contact* of hand, arm and cheek stroking. Given Catherine's apparent inability to vocalise, her poor vision and limited hearing, one can speculate that *social physical contact* would play an important role for her in any social interaction. This did indeed prove to be the case as shown by increased incidence of 'head turned towards' from a mean of 30 per cent during the baseline phase to 56 per cent in the intervention period. In the context of the limited movement Catherine had and the effort required to facilitate such movement of her head this 25 per cent increased incidence over such a short period represented major progress for Catherine.

Eye Contact

Even more significant was the emergence of *eye contact* after zero incidence for six baseline data points (see Figure 7.2). Staff commented that they could not recall Catherine ever previously engaging in any *eye contact*.

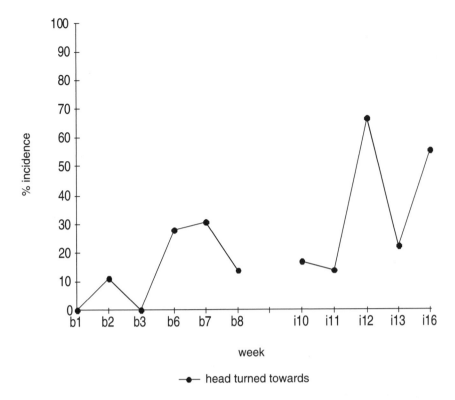

Figure 7.1 Percentage incidence of 'head turned towards' in close proximity situation

Video data from Intensive Interaction sessions

Generally, Catherine was lying on a support mat for these sessions, although in the later stages, when Liz had begun to elicit some engaged interaction, she sometimes positioned Catherine on her knee. The graphs in Figures 7.3 to 7.6 show that progress was beginning to be made in the Intensive Interaction sessions and it can only be left to speculation how much this would have developed over time. However, there are similar patterns emerging to those of the other children in the study, which suggests that further progress would have been likely.

The first of the graphs, in Figure 7.3, illustrates how the pattern of *no interactive behaviours* (the percentage of time when Catherine was in a passive state with her eyes either closed or in a fixed stare). This fell from an average score of 82 per cent in the baseline phase, to 56 per cent during the intervention phase.

As this reduction was taking place interactive behaviours were emerging. Progress was recorded in the *looking at/towards face* category as shown in Figure 7.4, where the mean value increased from 14 per cent in the baseline phase to 37 per cent in the intervention phase.

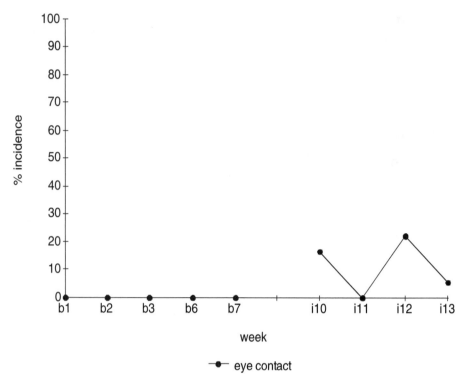

Figure 7.2 Percentage incidence of eye contact in social physical contact situation

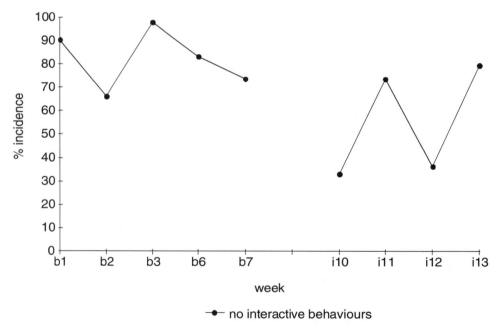

Figure 7.3 Percentage of no interactive behaviours

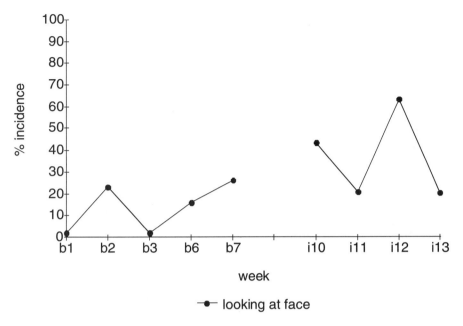

Figure 7.4 Percentage incidence of looking at face

Despite there being few data points, there are sufficient to show that *eye contact* did begin to emerge once Intensive Interaction sessions started (see Figure 7.5). This was a particularly significant step for Catherine. Staff remarked that they could never recall Catherine making *eye contact* and no previous record of this kind of communicative behaviour could be found.

The most compelling picture of progress emerging comes from the data for *joint focus*. Figure 7.6 shows a substantial increase in incidence – from a mean of 0.4 per cent to 28 per cent – clearly linked to the onset of intervention. The functional link is strengthened by the near zero score in the baseline phase being followed by an immediate and substantial surge of joint focus activity at the onset of Intensive Interaction.

Quality of life

The coded video data above provide only part of the picture of Catherine's story. Other important indicators of the effect Intensive Interaction was having on Catherine's quality of life can be gleaned from observations and staff comments noted in a research diary. Some of these comments refer to unexpected activities and developments that had not been coded for. One example is a communicative gesture that began to develop in response to Liz's playful interaction with Catherine. The only sound Catherine had been known to make prior to Intensive Interaction was

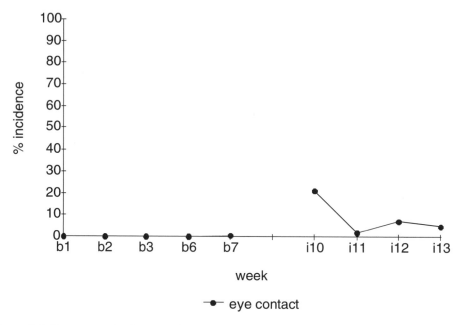

Figure 7.5 Percentage incidence of eye contact

a faint throaty moan. She had poor control of her mouth muscles and saliva dribbled uncontrollably out of whichever side her head was slumped on. Liz would often be playful about the saliva dribbles and started an imitative game, responding to Catherine's saliva dribbles by blowing small saliva bubbles back at her and making little noises. Sustained eye contact often accompanied this interchange. After several interchanges of playful bubble blowing producing an eye contact response, something new began to emerge. As Liz talked to Catherine and blew saliva bubbles, Catherine began to make a tutting noise with her tongue. Liz picked up on this immediately and imitated the tutting noise back. There were only a few Intensive Interaction sessions following this incident before Catherine died but they were punctuated with these little tutting exchanges. It developed into a game where Liz blew a raspberry close to Catherine's ear and Catherine responded with a smile and a 'saliva tut'. Liz said that she felt she was really connecting with Catherine in these moments. In the same way that she understood Catherine's screwing of her chin to be communicative (a sign of distress), Liz interpreted Catherine's tutting as communicative (a positive sign of interest and enjoyment). What was even more encouraging was that this tutting ability transferred into other behavioural situations external to the Intensive Interaction sessions including the home environment.

After Catherine's death, her mother wrote to express her gratitude that her daughter had been given the opportunity to participate in the Intensive Interaction project, describing their joy as a family in being able to 'connect' with Catherine.

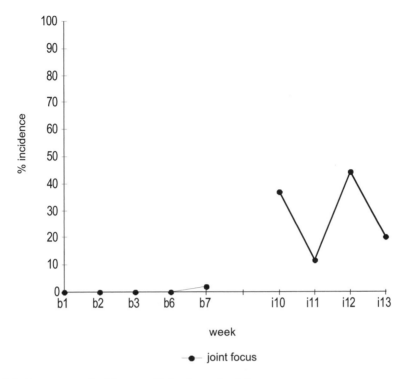

Figure 7.6 Percentage incidence of joint focus/activity

She wrote that those last few months were some of their happiest times together. We were able to give the family some video footage of Catherine enjoying Intensive Interaction with her teacher Liz. The video was alive with smiles, eye contact, warm physical interaction and the sound of Catherine using her tongue in a tutting sound as part of a playful imitative game.

CHAPTER 8

Jacob

Loss of continuity, organised self-involvement and progress surges

Introduction

Jacob's case study gives us an opportunity to discuss three important implementation issues: loss of continuity, progress surges and the effects of Intensive Interaction in situations where pupils' daily lives are dominated by what we record as 'organised self-involvement' (OSI) and what is generally known as 'stereotyped' behaviour. Our alternative language denotes our discomfort with some of the value judgements associated with stereotyped behaviours being purposeless and ripe for eradication (see Nind and Kellett 2002 for a fuller discussion).

About Jacob

Jacob was eight years old at the start of the project. He had severe generalised developmental delay compounded with physical impairments of kyphoscoliosis (curvature of the spine) and hypotania (floppiness) which meant he was unable to independently weight bear or sit for long periods of time. He was also epileptic. Jacob was at a pre-verbal stage of communication. He would often become distressed or frustrated and was prone to self-injurious behaviour of *banging* his head or elbow while *rocking* his upper body. Staff reported that he was not making any real progress and the class teacher remarked that she felt she had 'failed' Jacob.

There was a very positive response to introducing Intensive Interaction because the staff felt there was nothing to lose and everything to gain by trying a new approach. Emma, a teaching assistant, volunteered to work with Jacob and the class teacher supported her in this by facilitating daily release time for the Intensive Interaction sessions. Jacob remained on baseline for five weeks, represented by four data points (this period crossed a half-term break) and participated in Intensive Interaction for a further 42 weeks (represented by 15 data points). Unfortunately, Jacob's main Intensive Interaction partner, Emma, suffered a serious injury and was away from school for a period of 11 weeks (from week 13 to week 24). This was a most unfortunate occurrence because Jacob had already started to make good progress. Stretched resources meant that there was no other member of staff available to take over Emma's Intensive Interaction role. This is an example of what can happen when there is no team approach to Intensive Interaction – something stressed in all the literature on the approach, and stressed but not always achieved in this project. Despite best intentions and supportive gestures, such as the class teacher willingly facilitating release time for the Intensive Interaction sessions, Emma was effectively acting as a lone practitioner and there was no one else to step into the void created by her injury. A similar situation could have arisen if Emma had decided to move jobs or leave the area or for any one of a host of other reasons that might have resulted in loss of daily contact with Jacob.

During this period of absence staff commented that Jacob was 'pining' for Emma and missing his daily Intensive Interaction sessions. His social behaviour regressed to pre-intervention levels. This should not have been allowed to happen. We cannot stress strongly enough the importance of staff working in small teams rather than in isolation so that different staff and pupils learn to interact with each other rather than exclusive relationships being built. The less than ideal situation in Jacob's case study led to an emotional dependence and some distressing consequences when Intensive Interaction was suspended.

The only positive thing to come out of this unfortunate occurrence was an opportunity to analyse the effect of loss of continuity. It would have been grossly unethical to design a study that set out to withdraw an intervention anticipated to have a positive impact in order to measure its effect. However, since this situation arose naturally, and we were powerless to alter it, evaluating it could usefully further our knowledge and understanding of Intensive Interaction. The effect of loss of continuity due to staff sickness and to long school vacations is clearly evident in the illustrative data that follow. One of the important implications discussed is how quickly progress levels could be restored and whether some social behaviours took longer to be re-established than others.

Jacob's data

We have more data on the pupils than we can possibly report in this book. What we are doing is highlighting specific details in each case study that illuminate particular aspects of Intensive Interaction in terms of increasing our knowledge, improving our practice and analysing implementation factors. This chapter draws mainly on data from Jacob's Intensive Interaction sessions to support discussion related to three implementation issues: loss of continuity, OSI/'stereotyped' and self-injurious behaviours, and progress surges. Normal classroom data is only referred to in terms of the evidence it provides of sociability being transferred into

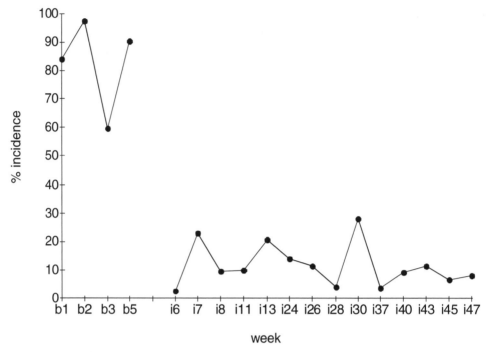

Figure 8.1 Percentage incidence of no interactive behaviours

other behavioural situations. Detailed analysis of these data can be found in Kellett (2001).

As outlined earlier, Jacob spent much of his school day in organised self-involvement, with some of his ritualistic behaviours also being self-injurious. His interaction with human beings at any level was minimal. This is illustrated in Figure 8.1 where percentage incidence scores for 'no interactive behaviours' are shown. Both baseline and intervention lines are bumpy and it is therefore helpful to compare average incidence across each phase. The incidence of Jacob not interacting was very high in the baseline phase, averaging 83 per cent. There was a substantial and immediate change once Intensive Interaction sessions began and over the period of intervention the average incidence of no interactive behaviours fell to 12 per cent.

We can examine what new behaviours were developing to fill this interactive void. One of the first social behaviours to emerge was that Jacob began to look at or towards Emma's face during the Intensive Interaction sessions. This increase is shown in Figure 8.2. There appears to be an immediate effect as soon as intervention started shown by the surge to 76 per cent incidence after the first week of Intensive Interaction sessions. This was mirrored by a second surge to 85 per cent at week 26 just after Intensive Interaction resumed following the 11-week gap when Emma was ill. These 'surges' of progress at early points in the use of Intensive

Interaction occurred across all six children but are most noticeable in Jacob's data because of the 'double start-up' scenario.

Close analysis of the Intensive Interaction videos and interviews with staff suggest that teacher enthusiasm was a factor in these early 'surges'. All the Intensive Interaction staff in the study reported their frustrations at wanting to get started but being constrained by the requirement for baseline data. This frustration increased the longer the baseline phase lasted and it is likely that some elements of Intensive Interaction may have subconsciously crept into the latter parts of baseline phase sessions (some rising end points were visible in several baseline phase data across the six pupils). When the time came for Intensive Interaction sessions to start, staff were highly motivated and buoyed up by enthusiasm and energy. Some of the best quality practice was observed in these early sessions.

As we have noted, it is also noticeable that towards the ends of terms progress tended to dip as staff became more and more exhausted from the physical and emotional strains of their teaching jobs. It is unlikely that the stress of working in schools is going to ease much in the short term, therefore we need to look at other ways of helping Intensive Interaction staff manage the quality of their practice. A good starting point is being aware that this is likely to happen – even to the most experienced and competent Intensive Interaction practitioners. None of us is superhuman and participating in Intensive Interaction takes physical and emotional energy. An Intensive Interaction Coordinator can be helpful in these situations. Sensitive monitoring by an IINCO should pick up any falling levels of quality interaction due to fatigue, staleness or depression and can initiate discussion about strategies to overcome some of the difficulties. If we remind ourselves that mutual pleasure is an important element of Intensive Interaction then it becomes clear that fatigue and depression are likely to have negative effects.

Early signs of social interaction

One of the earliest signs of social interaction to emerge was looking at or towards Emma's face. The slumping incidence that followed the 11-week break was rapidly reversed once Intensive Interaction sessions got under way again (see Figure 8.2).

The loss of 11 weeks of Intensive Interaction was unfortunate and staff reported that they thought Jacob was 'pining' for his sessions. Despite this setback the average incidence of looking at or towards Emma's face increased from 8 per cent in the baseline phase to 48 per cent in the intervention phase.

Another coded behaviour that showed early and sustained development was the ability to attend to a joint focus. This increased markedly from an average of 4 per cent in the baseline phase to 66 per cent over the period of Intensive Interaction, with the uneven but always higher pattern shown in Figure 8.3. The 'slumps' at vacation and illness periods are still visible, but only transiently and high joint focus scores were very quickly re-established.

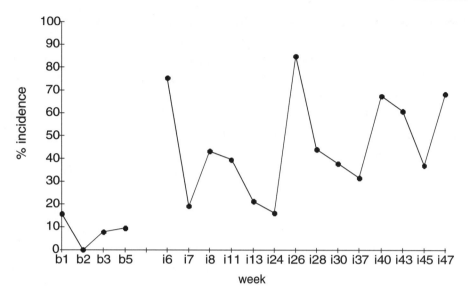

Figure 8.2 Percentage incidence of looking at/towards face

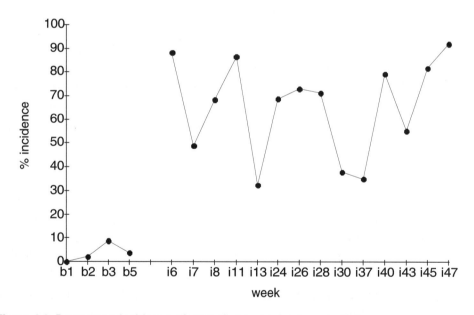

Figure 8.3 Percentage incidence of attending to a joint focus/activity

Later developments

Two coded behaviours that took a little longer to emerge were *eye contact* and the making or continuing of *social physical contact* (e.g. initiating or responding to the touching of a hand or a hug). However, the fact that both these socially interactive behaviours were completely absent from Jacob's communicative repertoire before

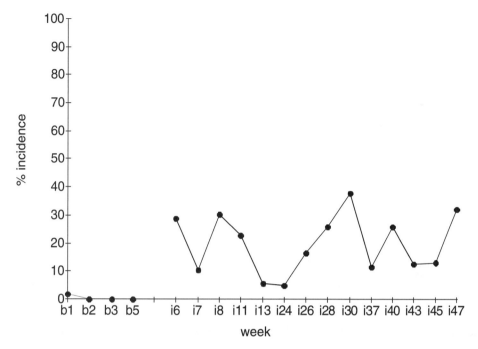

Figure 8.4 Percentage incidence of eye contact

the onset of Intensive Interaction makes these developments all the more significant. Staff could not recall a single incidence of eye contact or *social physical contact* prior to intervention. The graphs in Figures 8.4 and 8.5 depict zero baseline scores. It is noteworthy that these two social behaviours which took longer to emerge also seem to have taken longer to recover from vacation and teacher injury slumps (weeks 13–24 and 30–37) as can be seen in Figures 8.4 and 8.5.

Engagement

A final and crucially important behaviour coding was that of *engagement*. Figure 8.6 shows that Jacob responded rapidly to the Intensive Interaction approach and average incidence figures of 46 per cent for *engagement* during the intervention phase compared with 3 per cent in the baseline phase soundly endorse this.

The effect of Intensive Interaction on organised self-involvement

Jacob's organised self-involvement was coded into three categories: ritualistic *finger play*, *hand biting* and *rocking* (sometimes accompanied by *banging* of his head or elbow on hard surfaces). Incidence scores are shown in Table 8.1. An aggregate category was also calculated so that the total percentage of time spent could be analysed. This analysis does not reflect the value judgement that these 'stereotyped'

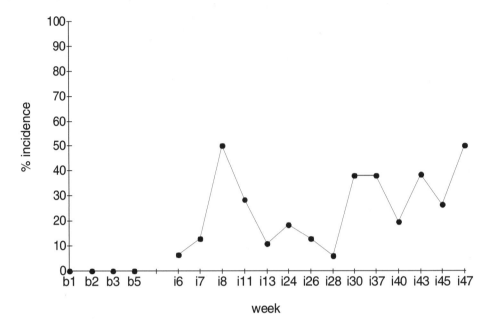

Figure 8.5 Percentage incidence of initiating or reciprocating social physical contact

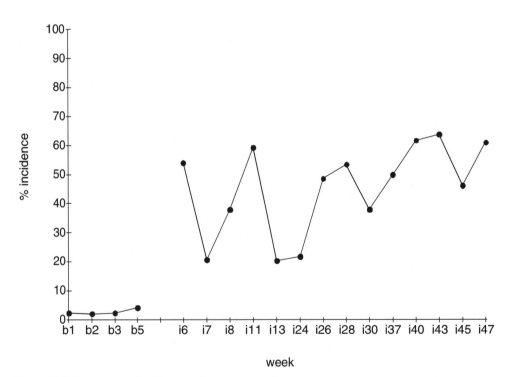

Figure 8.6 Percentage incidence of engagement

	rocking/ banging	finger play	hand biting	aggregate
b1	16	38	9.3	63.3
b2	12.3	34	18.7	65
b3	18.7	32.7	13.7	65.1
b5	14.7	35.7	23	73.4
i6	0	0	8.3	8.3
i7	2.7	1	5	8.7
i8	1	1	1.3	3.3
i11	0	7.3	4.3	11.6
i13	0	5.3	4	9.3
i24	0	1	3.3	4.3
i26	0	0.7	1.7	2.4
i28	0	0.7	0.3	1
i30	0	0	2	2
i37	0	2.3	0.7	3
i40	0	0	0	0
i43	0	0.3	3	3.3
i45	0	0	0	0
i47	0	0	0	0

Table 8.1 Percentage incidence scores for Jacob's stereotyped behaviours

behaviours lacked significance for Jacob, nor any devaluing of him because he spent his time in this way (see Nind and Kellett 2002). Rather, the purpose is to highlight that while Jacob was engaged in OSI it was hard for him to be interacting with his social environment. A reduction in stereotyped behaviours thus presented more opportunity for social interaction. It is important to stress that in the Intensive Interaction sessions Jacob *chose* to replace his stereotyped behaviours with others of a more socially communicative nature, presumably because he could and because he found these new behaviours more rewarding but no more threatening. Figure 8.7 shows the reduction in the aggregate incidence.

Transferability of communication progress

An important consideration in the evaluation of Intensive Interaction is whether or not the progress being made is transferable to other more generalised situations. For this reason, five-minute video clips of typical classroom behaviour were also filmed on the days when Intensive Interaction video data were being collected. These recordings were filmed during typical group activities and communicative behaviours coded

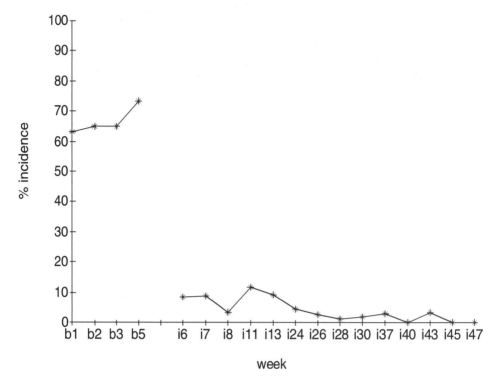

Figure 8.7 Percentage incidence of aggregate stereotyped behaviours

on a per second basis. Analysis of these data revealed that communication develop-ment did occur in these more general situations but not as quickly nor as strongly, suggesting that the Intensive Interaction was the optimum learning environment and nucleus of the progress which gradually spread into other behavioural situations. An example from the data that illustrates this point is the comparative rates of reduction in OSI in each of the two situations – Intensive Interaction sessions and classroom activity. During the baseline phase – before any Intensive Interaction had started – data for the classroom situation showed Jacob spending all of his time occupied in OSI. This situation did begin to change after the introduction of Intensive Interaction. As can be seen in Figure 8.8, reductions were not as great as during Intensive Interaction sessions themselves, but nevertheless show a substantial reduc-tion over a longer period of time. The 100 per cent incidence before the introduction of Intensive Interaction, coupled with staff observations about Jacob spending the majority of his day in ritualistic, self-absorbed behaviours, gives a strong indication that the subsequent reduction was functionally linked to his participation in Intensive Interaction.

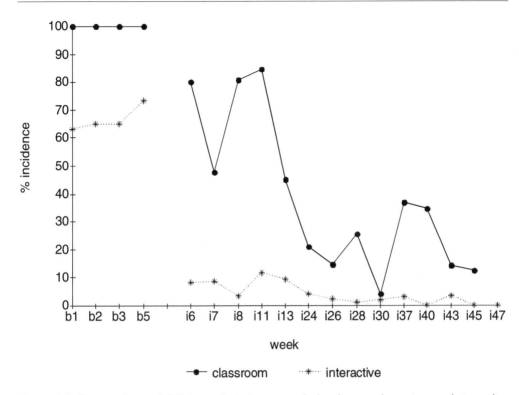

Figure 8.8 Comparison of OSI in typical classroom behaviour and one-to-one interactive behaviour situations

Published assessment schedule data

Observation data from the video footage were triangulated with two published assessment schedules, the Kiernan and Reid (1987) Pre-Verbal Communication Schedule and an adaptation of Brazelton's (1984) Cuddliness Scale. The measurements were taken at the beginning and end of the baseline, then at a probe point when the intervention phase had been running for an equal time to the baseline phase, and finally at the end of the project. The schedules recorded no progress in the five weeks of baseline. Kiernan and Reid's Short Score Pre-Verbal Communication Schedule uses 175 descriptors of communication behaviour. Figure 8.9 illustrates the total percentage of attainments (out of the maximum of 175) at the four measurement points.

Jacob was able to achieve 14 per cent of the pre-verbal communication descriptors at the beginning of baseline and this figure had not changed at the end of baseline. After five weeks the first intervention probe assessment was taken and Jacob's achievements had increased to 17 per cent of the Pre-Verbal Communication Schedule. At the end of the study this figure had risen to 57 per cent.

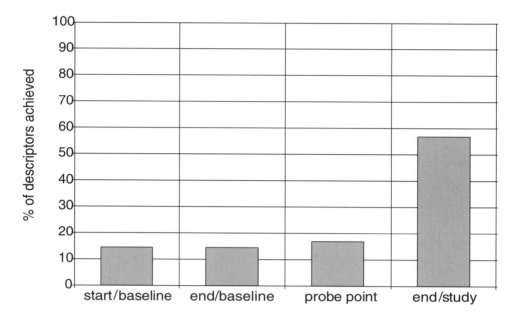

Figure 8.9 Percentage of PVCS attainments achieved at the four specified points in the study

Physical sociability scale

This assessment was based on an adaptation of Brazelton's (1984) Cuddliness Scale and designed to measure physical sociability as a form of communication. Table 8.2 shows Jacob's progress.

Jacob's baseline scores show that he responded passively to *social physical contact*, neither actively resisting nor participating. After five weeks of Intensive Interaction, at the intervention probe, this situation had moved up to point 5 on the scale – *usually relaxes and moulds when first held*. By the end of the project Jacob had progressed to the top of the scale where he himself was initiating the *social physical contact*.

Staff and researcher observations

Another important source of data that contributes to Jacob's case study is observation from staff and researcher about events that were not captured on video. One such example is Emma's description of how Jacob learned to speak his first word, 'yum'. She described how they would play games at meal-times. In these teasing, anticipation games Emma would recite '*yum yummy yum yum*' as part of the game repertoire. After a few weeks of using this phrase Jacob began to smack

1. **Actively** resists being held (e.g. stiffens, thrashes, pushes away)		
2. Resists being held **most** but **not all** of the time		
3. Does not resist being held but **does not participate** (lies passively)	*1*	*2*
4. Will **eventually** relax and mould into being held but only after a lot of encouragement		
5. Will **usually** relax and mould when **first** held	*3*	
6. **Always** relaxes and moulds when **first** held		
7. Relaxes, moulds and **actively turns head towards** interactive partner		
8. **All of above plus** initiates physical contact such as clinging or grasping	*4*	

1 = beginning of baseline   *2* = end of baseline   *3* = intervention probe   *4* = end of study

Table 8.2 Physical Sociability Assessment Scale (adapted from Brazelton 1984)

his lips and uttered his very first word *yum.* The research diary notes a similar occurrence happening in the typical classroom environment during 'drink and snack' time. A drink and a handful of raisins had been put on the table in front of Jacob. It was common practice that a member of staff would feed these to Jacob because he did not have the fine motor control to pick up the raisins or control the beaker. The member of staff was called away and meanwhile Jacob tried to pick up the raisins himself. Although he frequently got one in range of his fingers, he could not manage to pick one up. He became increasingly frustrated by this lack of success and started to rock and wail in distress. When this failed to gain the attention of the busy member of staff, Jacob's wailing began to be punctuated with *yum yum . . . yum yum . . . yum . . .*, a clear attempt on his part to communicate his needs.

Discussions with staff showed unanimous acknowledgement of the immense progress Jacob had made since starting out on his Intensive Interaction journey:

- his self-injurious behaviours all but disappeared;
- the OSI behaviours such as finger flapping greatly reduced;
- he became much more alert and aware of his peers and environment;
- he was able to participate in group activities.

Staff were also of the opinion that Jacob had become a much happier child. They had discovered a delightfully humorous, mischievous side to his character they had not known before. Furthermore he was making great progress in his ability to communicate needs and emotions. The overall feeling was that Jacob had progressed from being a 'hard to reach' child, who spent the majority of his time in self-injurious, stereotyped behaviours, to a happy, socially interactive child who could participate in joint activities, engage in purposeful social interaction and was beginning to use some formal communication skills.

Implications for practice

The surges of progress near the beginning of Intensive Interaction start-up periods are important in three respects. Firstly it suggests that there are real benefits to be gained when practitioners are fresh and enthusiastic. This has planning implications for managers wanting to introduce Intensive Interaction into schools for the first time. It is advisable to do this at the beginning of a term – September is ideal because staff have had the benefit of the summer vacation to recover their energy levels. Intensive Interaction Coordinators can monitor levels of physical and emotional well-being among staff. Once again, a team approach can do much to reduce negative effects. Sharing the load, supporting one another and being prepared to stand in for colleagues should the need arise characterises best practice.

Secondly the surges of progress suggest that there might also be 'pupil enthusiasm' levels to consider. More research is needed in this area but it is reasonable to speculate that a sudden change of style to contingent responding which values even the smallest actions of the individual is likely to be met with initial surges of enthusiasm by pupils.

Thirdly the degree of 'surge' appears to vary according to different types of social behaviour. The most immediate and substantial surges were recorded for behaviours such as *visual scanning* and *looking at face*, while behaviours like *eye contact* and *contingent vocalisation* were not affected to the same degree. Also when the 11-week suspension period occurred, it was these first mentioned behaviours that were more quickly re-established than the latter. This gives further credence to a hypothesis of a 'continuum' of sociability development linked to Intensive Interaction intervention. This could be useful information for managers and those coordinating Intensive Interaction at a whole-school level. Different skills and personalities suggest that some staff will be better at certain types of interaction than others (for example, communication by touch or vocal imitation) and might be more effective at different stages of this development continuum. It may be worth exploring how different team combinations of particular skills and experience can be optimised.

Most importantly, Jacob's case study demonstrates that loss of continuity can have damaging emotional consequences and how important it is to think through a plan of action before starting Intensive Interaction. Once again a good team approach can help prevent many undesirable situations arising.

Continuity checklist for coordinators

The following continuity checklist for IINCOs or other key staff might be useful:

- Are staff genuinely willing to participate? There is a higher chance of drop-out if an element of coercion has been involved.
- Has full training been given? Was the training recent enough? Is top-up training needed?
- Are several members of staff working together as a team? Are there opportunities for team reflections, team brainstorms, team support networks?
- Is the physical and emotional well-being of staff being considered? Are there opportunities for staff to talk through any personal or professional difficulties they might be having that could affect the quality of their practice?
- Has the timing of vacations been considered with regard to start-up times?
- Are there contingency plans for staff moving on? Is the emotional well-being of pupils at risk from over-dependency?

Summary

Jacob's story raises our awareness about the negative impact that loss of continuity can have on overall progress. It has also shown us that the early stages of Intensive Interaction are a particularly vulnerable time when continuity is vital. There is less likelihood of regression once the approach has had a chance to become established. Social behaviours that emerge earliest are less prone to regression than those that take longer to emerge. Jacob's story has also enabled us to reflect on how we can respond more positively to behaviours construed as stereotyped.

CHAPTER 9

Bernadette

Two steps forward, one step back

Introduction

This chapter has a slightly different format from the others in this part. It deals with what happens when progress associated with Intensive Interaction is affected by other impairments that cause concomitant deterioration so that overall progress is halted or impeded. In Bernadette's case the outcome of Intensive Interaction was affected by the onset of Rett syndrome and its diagnosis made part-way through the study. Difficulties of measuring progress in these circumstances are discussed, dangers of negative attitudes addressed and strategies for remaining positive and focused are explored. Bernadette's study is also another example of how emotional well-being impacts on optimum outcomes.

About Bernadette

Bernadette was approaching four years old at the start of the project and had spent two terms at an integrated nursery school. Staff commented that Bernadette appeared to 'live in a world of her own', wanting no contact with them or her peers. She made no eye contact and if allowed the freedom of the nursery unit or the play-ground, would spend her time walking in constant circles, often pushing an object such as a toy pushchair or a toy scooter as she did so. Staff described her as a silent little girl who did not vocalise. She had no physical problems other than needing to wear spectacles to correct her vision. Gail, a learning support assistant, took on the role of Intensive Interaction partner.

Data from typical classroom behaviour

The nursery consisted of a large open-plan area with an adjacent small activity room. The typical classroom behaviour video footage was filmed in the large open-plan space during 'free choosing time'. The Intensive Interaction sessions took place in the activity room. An additional code of *wandering* was adopted for Bernadette to describe her *wandering* about without apparent purpose. This code plus one for *finger play* represented Bernadette's organised self-involvement.

Behaviour code data from the typical classroom situation reveal very limited sociability and communication skills. Her progress was confined to some increased incidence in *visual scanning* and *purposeful involvement with a toy*. The increased incidence of *visual scanning* and becoming more aware of her environment did have a parallel reduction in the incidence of OSI initially. However, subsequent to this initial progress, OSI started to increase again and in the latter stages of the project incidence of *visual scanning* also became very patchy. This was quite puzzling because no similar increase was happening in Bernadette's Intensive Interaction sessions and nothing similar had happened in the typical classroom data of the other five participants in the study. The fact that some progress from the Intensive Interaction sessions had already started to transfer to Bernadette's typical classroom behaviour evidenced in the data for *visual scanning* and *purposeful involvement with an object* made this pattern all the more disappointing. Staff reported other bizarre behaviour that had not been caught on video, principally bouts of high-pitched screeching. Bernadette underwent further diagnostic tests and in the last term of the study it was confirmed that she had Rett syndrome. One of the characteristics of Rett syndrome is a compulsive, ritualistic playing with or wringing of the hands (Sandberg *et al.* 2000). Close examination of the initial progress Bernadette had made, and comparative data from the other five participants who sustained a consistent reduction in ritualistic OSI behaviour, suggest that the Rett syndrome may have been the primary cause of raised OSI levels. Further credence is given to this hypothesis when the OSI data are separated out into the two codes of *finger play* and *wandering* as shown in Figure 9.1, revealing a steady and sustained reduction in one and an initial reduction that was not sustained in the other.

Data from Intensive Interaction sessions

Analysis of these data is particularly powerful for our evaluative purposes. They indicate that even with the onset of Rett syndrome characteristics, good social and communicative progress was still being made in these sessions.

Data from the baseline phase show an average of 90 per cent of the time was devoid of any socially interactive behaviour. Video footage shows Bernadette turning her back on Gail and not responding to her name or any other effort by Gail to engage her. By contrast data from the intervention phase show that the incidence of no interactive behaviours fell to an average of 19 per cent and began to be replaced by socially communicative behaviours.

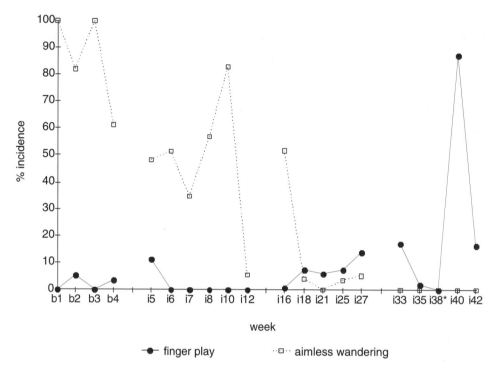

Figure 9.1 Percentage incidence for OSI behaviours of finger play and aimless wandering

Additional information from the research diary is relevant here. Bernadette's interactive partner, Gail, made a very enthusiastic and skilful start to Intensive Interaction sessions and was rewarded by some remarkable early progress from Bernadette. A tragic incident happened in Gail's personal life towards the end of the first term, which very probably had a major impact on her performance as an interactive partner. This pattern of difficulties in the life of a staff member affecting pupil progress was also evident for Clare and Sam (see Chapter 5).

Gail admitted that she found it difficult to be happy and playful in the Intensive Interaction sessions with Bernadette during this time. Absence of mutual pleasure (Bretherton *et al.* 1979) and the depressed state of the adult interactive partner (Clark and Seifer 1983) contributed to a partial breakdown of the Intensive Interaction. It is important to keep in mind the two sets of additional information described above regarding Gail's depressed emotional state for part of the intervention phase and the latterly onset of Bernadette's Rett syndrome characteristics. The first of these, affecting weeks 8 to 12, we have called 'factor G', and the second, affecting weeks 33 to the end of the study, we have called 'factor R'.

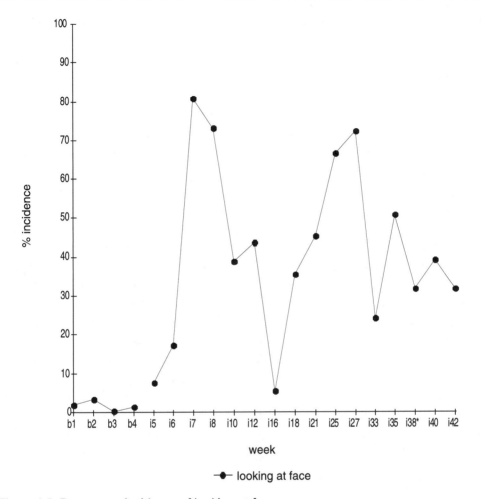

Figure 9.2 Percentage incidence of looking at face

Bernadette begins to look at Gail

One of the first communicative behaviours to emerge was *looking at/towards face.* If we analyse these data we can see the progress that was being made and assess what impact the 'G' and 'R' factors were having. Data are presented in graph form in Figure 9.2.

The first thing to note is that the baseline is relatively flat with a negligible average incidence of 2 per cent. These scores reflect staff comments that Bernadette hardly ever looked towards them, usually away from them or at the floor. The baseline period was followed by a spectacularly rapid increase in the incidence of Bernadette looking at or towards Gail's face in the first three weeks of Intensive Interaction. These data are supported by video footage showing Bernadette sitting on Gail's knee with face-to-face contact and wonderfully close social interchange including quality eye contact. 'Factor G' (Gail's personal tragedy, weeks 8–12) coincides with an equally spectacular fall in the incidence of *looking at face*. A school vacation occurred between weeks 13 and 16 when Bernadette did not participate in any Intensive Interaction so by the start of the second term, week 16, incidence had regressed almost to baseline levels.

After the Christmas vacation (week 16) Gail had overcome the worst of her difficulties and her positive state appears to be reflected in a renewed surge in incidence scores for *looking at face*, rising rapidly again and peaking at 72 per cent in week 27. The onset of the characteristics of Rett syndrome ('Factor R', weeks 33 to the end of the study) coincide with a second fall in the incidence scores for *looking at face*. It is interesting that this regression is not as great as the 'Factor G' regression suggesting that emotional well-being had the greater negative impact. This is a crucially important finding. It informs us about the importance of staying positive in the face of demoralising developments. Yes, we may have to accept that some other impairment might impede the good progress we are making through Intensive Interaction, but we would be unwise to abandon the approach because of that. In Bernadette's case study the progress achieved through skilful Intensive Interaction was greater than the regression ascribed to characteristics of Rett syndrome.

Two steps forward and one step back is a better outcome than two steps forward and two or more steps back. Furthermore the stronger levels of regression that were evident during Gail's emotionally depressed state tell us that much progress is actually in our own hands. Staying positive, staying fresh and staying emotionally healthy is the best way to combat regressions from debilitating impairments that may occur and worsen before or during Intensive Interaction.

Bernadette begins to smile

Scores for the behaviour code of *contingent happy/smiling face* are represented in graph form in Figure 9.3. The flat baseline phase and average of 0.2 per cent is a strong position from which to claim a functional link between Intensive Interaction and the increased incidence of *contingent happy/smiling face* over the intervention phase which varied from a mean of 9 per cent in term one, dipping to a 5 per cent mean in term 2 and then rising to a 16 per cent mean in term three.

Eye contact

Incidence scores for *eye contact* follow a similar pattern to those for *looking at face* and are represented graphically in Figure 9.4 where the weeks are separated out into termly blocks so that the effect of vacations can be more easily identified. The absolute zero rating of the baseline phase concurs with staff comments about Bernadette never engaging in *eye contact*, indeed hardly ever looking in the general direction of people's faces. After three weeks of Intensive Interaction this position had changed considerably with an unusually high incidence peak of 60 per cent. There was a

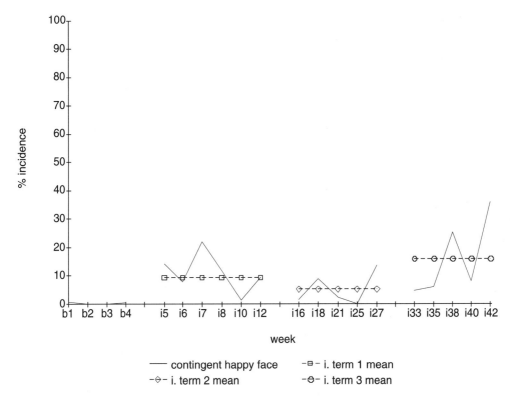

Figure 9.3 Percentage incidence of contingent happy/smiling face with termly mean values

sharp fall in the latter stages of term 1, coinciding with 'Factor G', which fell further over the fallow period of the school holiday. Once Intensive Interaction sessions got going again and Gail was more herself, the incidence scores started to rise steeply for the second term, regressing during the next vacation, but then not getting going again convincingly in the third term.

There are three possible explanations for the sustained regression in the third term. One is that the incidence of *eye contact* was adversely affected by Rett syndrome characteristics, a second is that Intensive Interaction was simply not effective in the longer term and a third that some interpersonal breakdown occurred similar to 'Factor G'. The historical log and researcher diary preclude any further relationship breakdown and comparisons with *eye contact* scores from other participants do not show dipping longer-term scores, so the third term regression is more likely to have been due to the progressive nature of Rett syndrome. In speculating whether or not Intensive Interaction might have become ineffective over the longer term, one only has to look again at the baseline phase average of 0 per cent to realise that a longer-term regression to an average incidence of 15 per cent still represents a substantial development.

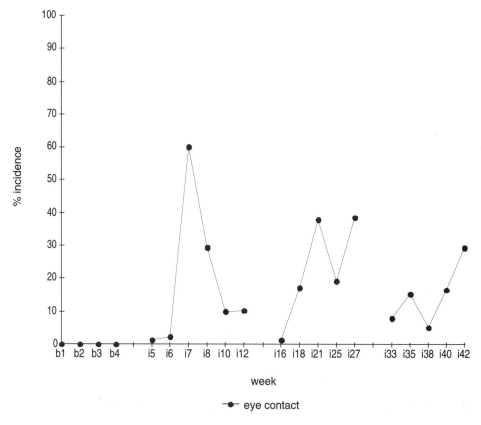

Figure 9.4 Percentage incidence of eye contact

Staying positive

Another reason to stay very positive when faced with setbacks like Bernadette's Rett syndrome is that the progress outcomes that are most affected are those closely linked to the characteristics of the condition. In Bernadette's case this related to the increasingly ritualistic activity with her hands. Other developments such as *contingent vocalisation* may be less affected and it may be possible to adjust the Intensive Interaction sessions to maximise those socially interactive moments least likely to be affected by the Rett syndrome. One of the successful strategies Gail adopted was that she picked up contingently on Bernadette's liking for action songs and rhymes. This led to some quality *contingent vocalisation* including three monosyllabic words. *Contingent vocalisation* was defined in the protocol as a sound(s) or word(s) that was contingent upon an interactive aspect of the session and was ascribed communicative intent. There were only very small levels of development of this with the other participants and it was viewed as a higher order communication skill that might develop as participants progressed nearer to formal speech or signing. It is particu-

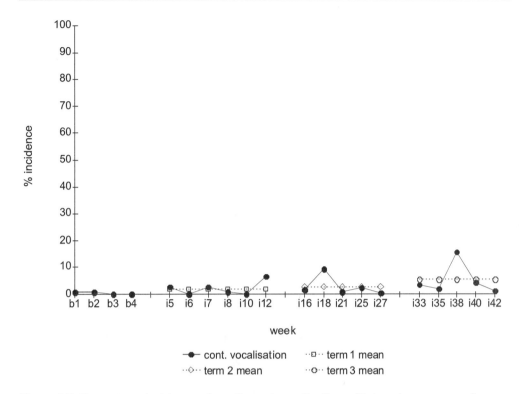

Figure 9.5 Percentage incidence of contingent vocalisation with termly average values

larly interesting that in Bernadette's case this was one of the behaviours that developed consistently and was sustained over the longer term despite the difficulties mentioned above. Incidence scores with termly mean values are shown in Figure 9.5. The zero baseline is contrasted with steadily increasing incidence scores over the three terms averaging 2 per cent, 3 per cent and 5 per cent consecutively. These incidence figures may seem modest in comparison to some of the higher scores witnessed in behaviours such as *looking at face* and *joint focus*, but these small percentages translate in real world terms to developments of rich quality with imitative vocalisations including three distinct words: *there, yeah* and *hup* (up).

Attending to a joint focus

In spite of all the difficulties associated with Bernadette's case study there are two areas where outstanding progress was achieved. The first of these is the ability to attend to a *joint focus* or activity with the interactive partner. Incidence scores are shown in Figure 9.6. There are several points of analysis with regard to Bernadette's ability to attend to a *joint focus*. The first is that 'Factor G' is plainly evident in Figure 9.6 between weeks 8 and 12 and compounded by a slump at week 16 after

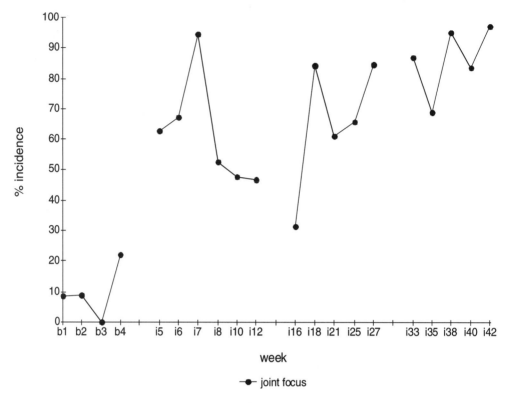

Figure 9.6 Percentage incidence of joint focus/activity

the school holiday. It is also evident that 'Factor R' is entirely missing. The overall incidence of joint focus in the intervention phase was very high, as tended to be the case with the other participants. In Bernadette's case it averaged 71 per cent compared to her baseline phase average of 10 per cent. It is interesting that even with such high incidence scores, this progress was still vulnerable to a 'Factor G' slump, but not a 'Factor R' slump. This concurs with earlier observations and suggests that the kind of emotional depression experienced by Gail seems to be more powerful and far-reaching in its negative influence on the efficacy of the approach than the impact of the progressive Rett syndrome. The success of Intensive Interaction in developing joint focus was noted across all six participants. Where a debilitating condition, like Rett syndrome, is likely to increase ritualistic, self-absorbed activity, Intensive Interaction seems to be a powerful way of engaging that individual, presenting them with more interesting, interactive opportunities that may actually *reduce* some of the negative impact of the impairment on sociability and communication.

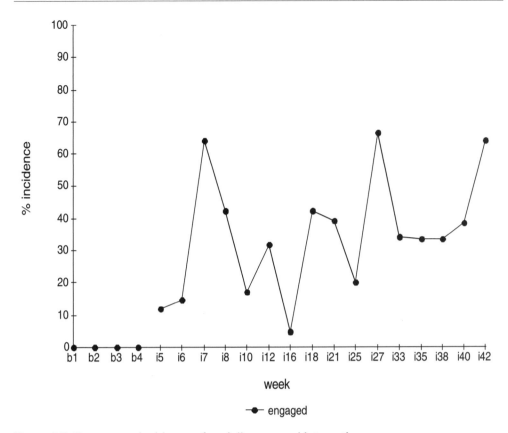

Figure 9.7 Percentage incidence of socially engaged interaction

Engagement

This point is endorsed by the data for the coding of 'engagement' shown in Figure 9.7. Once again there is a completely zero rated baseline phase, which strengthens the claim that progress was functionally linked to the onset of Intensive Interaction. The lowest point in the intervention phase appears to correlate with all the conditions described above for 'Factor G'. Apart from these two points on the graph, the picture depicted is an endorsement of sustained development throughout the Intensive Interaction phase progressing from no *engagement* in the baseline phase to a mean incidence of 35 per cent.

Even more interesting is a direct comparison of the data for ritualistic *finger play* in typical classroom behaviour and Intensive Interaction sessions. Earlier in this chapter we showed how the incidence of this kind of self-involved *finger play* rose in line with the developing characteristics of Rett syndrome. In the typical classroom situation Bernadette spent much of her time pushing a wheeled toy around in circles. Because she had to hold on to the toy this would have excluded much of

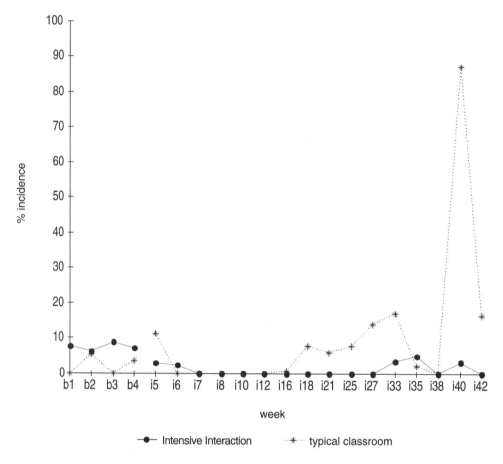

Figure 9.8 Incidence of ritualistic finger play in Intensive Interaction and typical classroom situations

the *finger play*. As the characteristics of Rett syndrome developed the ritualistic *finger play* increased and she spent less time pushing a toy. She still wandered around but wringing her hands and playing with her fingers as she did so. In the Intensive Interaction any increases in *finger play* at the same stage were much slighter by comparison (see Figure 9.8). Within the specific context of the Intensive Interaction sessions, the baseline phase average incidence of ritualistic *finger play* of 8 per cent gradually reduced down to zero. This was sustained for 19 weeks, before it began to rise again in the final term between weeks 33 and 42 but only to an average of 2 per cent. In view of all the other evidence of Bernadette's case study it seems likely that the small increase in the third term was due to the progressive nature of Rett syndrome and the increase may have been partially nullified by Intensive Interaction.

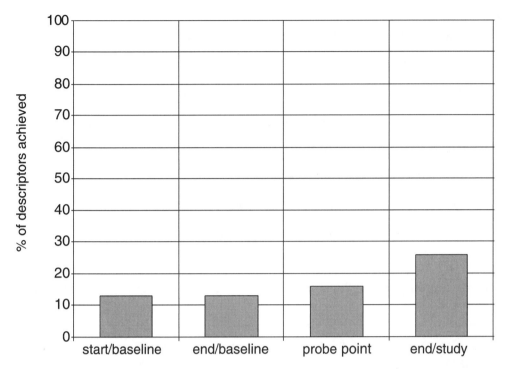

Figure 9.9 Percentage of PVCS attainments achieved at the four specified points in the study

Kiernan and Reid Pre-Verbal Communication Schedule

As in the other case studies featured in this part, the data were triangulated by two other assessments, the Kiernan and Reid Pre-Verbal Communication Schedule (PVCS) and the Physical Sociability Assessment Scale. The measurements were taken at the beginning and end of the baseline and then at a probe point when Bernadette had been on the intervention phase for the same number of weeks as baseline phase, and finally at the end of the project. No progress was measured in the four weeks of baseline therefore the progress that was made over the intervention phase is more likely to be linked to the introduction of Intensive Interaction rather than natural maturation. Figure 9.9 illustrates the total percentage of attainments at the four predetermined points.

Figure 9.9 shows that Bernadette had only achieved 13 per cent of the Pre-Verbal Communication Schedule at the start and end of baseline phase. She had made a small degree of progress by the fourth week of intervention, 16 per cent, when the probe point was taken. By the end of the study she had achieved 26 per cent of the pre-verbal schedule. This was modest compared to the achievements of some of the other participants, but nevertheless represented a doubling of her achievements

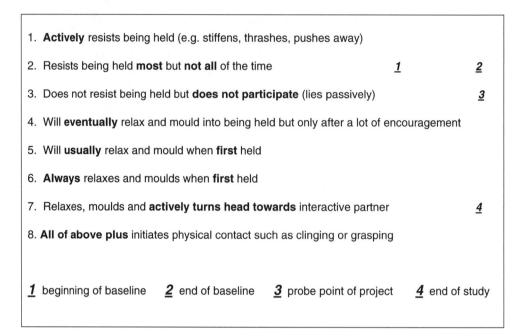

1. **Actively** resists being held (e.g. stiffens, thrashes, pushes away)

2. Resists being held **most** but **not all** of the time   _1_   _2_

3. Does not resist being held but **does not participate** (lies passively)   _3_

4. Will **eventually** relax and mould into being held but only after a lot of encouragement

5. Will **usually** relax and mould when **first** held

6. **Always** relaxes and moulds when **first** held

7. Relaxes, moulds and **actively turns head towards** interactive partner   _4_

8. **All of above plus** initiates physical contact such as clinging or grasping

_1_ beginning of baseline   _2_ end of baseline   _3_ probe point of project   _4_ end of study

Figure 9.10 Physical Sociability Assessment Scale (adapted from Brazelton 1984 and Nind 1993)

from the start of the project and included the beginning of formal communication in her use of three words.

Physical Sociability Assessment Scale

The second published assessment schedule, shown in Figure 9.10, illustrates the communicative progress of physical sociability made by Bernadette. At the beginning and end of the baseline phase, Bernadette resisted being held by members of staff and any attempts to cuddle her. After four weeks of Intensive Interaction, this position changed slightly to one where she tolerated this form of physical social communication in a passive way but without any attempt to participate. By the end of the project Bernadette was very comfortable with *social physical contact* and had moved up to point 7 on the scale where she actively moulded and relaxed into a cuddle and turned her head towards her interactive partner in a clear attempt to communicate.

Summary

In quantitative terms, Bernadette appeared to make less progress than her co-participants. However, conversations with participating staff give a strong impression that the social and communication developments she made had a considerable impact on their daily interaction with her and they considered her a different child altogether after three terms of Intensive Interaction. At the start of the project she apparently 'lived in a world of her own', did not interact at any level with her peers or staff and spent much of her time in a seemingly ritualistic 'wandering'. By the end of the study staff reported getting wonderful eye contact from her, lots of hugs and cuddles and she was much more willing to sit still and enjoy a joint focus activity with a member of staff. Amid all this positive social and communicative development, Bernadette acquired three words in her vocabulary. Despite the onset of the characteristics of Rett syndrome, considerable progress was still achieved with Intensive Interaction. Progressing two steps forward and one step back still represents movement in the right direction, albeit at a necessarily slower pace.

CHAPTER 10

Shane

Micro-politics, senior management support and coordination

Introduction

Shane's story illustrates some complex implementation issues that can arise out of the micro-politics in a classroom. Micro-politics that interfere with optimum outcomes are not unique to Intensive Interaction nor to schools in general. Most organisations have to face difficulties of this nature at one time or another. Where human beings work together on a daily basis there are bound to be occasions when particular strengths, weaknesses and personality traits cause friction. Undercurrents of dissatisfaction, pockets of resistance and overt or covert subversion are all damaging to teamwork, to morale and to optimum outcomes. In this chapter we look at the effect of classroom micro-politics in conjunction with low levels of senior management support and discuss how good coordination can minimise the negative impacts of both.

About Shane

Shane was aged six at the start of the project. He had no physical difficulties other than having sluggish movements but his learning difficulties were severe and he was at a very early pre-verbal stage of communication. Staff described him as passive, never getting involved in any peer activities and often lying down on the floor or putting his head down on the table as if he were constantly tired and sleepy. He would spend much of his time chewing items of his clothing or other items he found lying around. Staff found it difficult to engage him in any form of social interaction.

Micro-politics

There are particular circumstances surrounding Shane's case study that need clarification at the outset. Shortly after the project began Shane's class teacher was taken ill. A learning support assistant, Jane, who had agreed to be Shane's Intensive Interaction partner, was asked to take on additional administrative responsibilities for a period of several months to support a stream of short-term supply teachers who covered the absence. This meant that she was unable to continue with the Intensive Interaction project and there was a gap of several weeks before another partner could be found. Eventually a learning support colleague, Fleur, volunteered. Because of the stop-start nature, the fact that Shane had not progressed beyond a few weeks of the baseline phase and in consideration of the gap that had ensued in the interim, we took the decision to start again with a new baseline phase. This late start meant that only 43 weeks of data could be fitted into the time frame, which translated into six weeks of baseline and 37 weeks of intervention, represented by five baseline points and 16 intervention points.

Jane remained ideologically committed to Intensive Interaction and in practice the two members of staff worked together as a team for the Intensive Interaction. Fleur did the majority of the Intensive Interaction sessions, Jane helped out wherever possible and they discussed progress together. With the rapid turnover of stop-gap supply cover it was the learning support assistants who were providing the stability and curriculum impetus in the class. They had more influence than ever before in the management of the classroom. Jane's and Fleur's enthusiasm for Intensive Interaction infected the third learning support assistant in the class and soon all three of them were doing Intensive Interaction with several children, not just Shane. This state of affairs was the closest match to Nind's (1993) original study when a whole-team approach to Intensive Interaction was adopted.

It was very exciting to witness the spread of Intensive Interaction in this way. For an hour each morning the three assistants operated a room management system whereby two of them supported the supply teacher working with the whole class, while the third participated in an Intensive Interaction session with one pupil. They alternated roles so that pupils and learning support staff all got opportunities to practise Intensive Interaction. Team cooperation and team commitment fuelled their enthusiasm and short spontaneous bursts of Intensive Interaction began to happen at other times too, whenever opportunities presented themselves. It felt very much as if Intensive Interaction had become an integral part of the classroom ethos.

This lasted for three months until the class teacher returned. Quite understandably she wanted to re-establish her own classroom routines and take up the leadership reins again. This meant that the Intensive Interaction rota system not only ceased, but daily sessions became more and more irregular as the class teacher increasingly prioritised other activities. Fleur found it frustrating not knowing from day to day whether she would be able to have her Intensive Interaction session with Shane, to the point that she and Jane would 'sneak' (their word) Intensive Interaction sessions into lunch-time, nappy-changing-time and play-time – availing themselves of any fleeting opportunity to make up for lost time.

We need to deconstruct some of the classroom micro-politics here to try to understand what was happening and what impact this was having on Intensive Interaction. Originally, when the project was first proposed, the class teacher had not been ideologically opposed to Intensive Interaction, nor is there any suggestion that she became so during the lifetime of the project. The micro-politics at work were more about asserting control and taking ownership of pupil progress. There may even have been an element of professional jealousy in that Shane's visible progress was being attributed to something into which the class teacher had had no input. With these undercurrents of tension one can understand how the Intensive Interaction could easily become the focus – or scapegoat – of the conflict and the approach become subverted.

This kind of subversion is not uncommon at the implementation stage of an innovation (see Chapter 3) and it can happen at several levels with Intensive Interaction:

- time/event 'blocking' – making it difficult for Intensive Interaction sessions to happen;
- observation 'blocking' – consciously or unconsciously not noticing progress;
- progress 'hijack' – attributing progress made to causes other than Intensive Interaction;
- adjustment 'blocking' – not acknowledging that curricula adjustments are required to match progress made.

To a lesser or greater extent all of these levels were at work within the micro-politics of this case study. The learning support assistants felt that Shane's progress was not being acknowledged and his curriculum was not being adapted to his new communicative abilities. They feared he was getting bored and that this was beginning to lead to some sociability regression. There is some support for this theory in the data. Analysis shows there were substantially sharper differences between typical classroom behaviour and interactive behaviour in the Intensive Interaction sessions than was the case with the other five pupils in the study. Typical classroom behaviour was in the jurisdiction of the class teacher whereas the Intensive Interaction sessions were not. The implications of this are important and will be referred to as happening in the Intensive Interaction sessions.

Findings related to the Intensive Interaction sessions

One of the exciting aspects of Shane's case study is the scale of progress that he made in the Intensive Interaction sessions. Jane's and Fleur's strength of belief that Intensive Interaction was making a real difference to Shane's sociability encouraged them to do some of these sessions in their own break-times when continuity was threatened. This is evidence of the self-sustaining nature of the approach. The

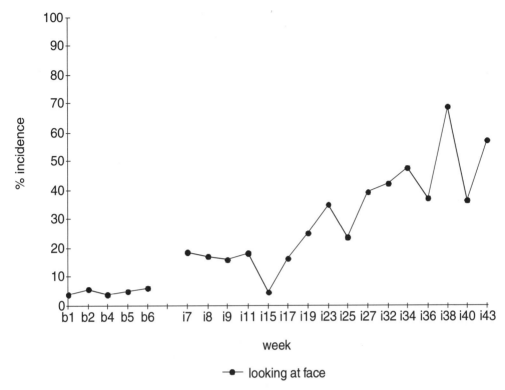

Figure 10.1 Percentage incidence of looking at/towards face

increased incidence of social communication behaviours was on a particularly large scale. Those socially interactive behaviours that proved harder to develop in other pupils, such as initiating social contact, did begin to happen for Shane. Figures 10.1 to 10.5 illustrate the levels of progress that were made.

Detailed analysis of the individual coding has already been undertaken in Sam's and Harriet's case studies and it is not appropriate to reproduce that level of detail again here, especially as substantial progress is self-evident in the graphs. However, a few specific comments on features unique to this case study are worthy of note.

The data in Figure 10.3 for *reciprocating social physical contact* chart an interesting picture. There is virtually no immediate change in level when Intensive Interaction begins. It took five weeks before a breakthrough came, but when it did come it was followed by very rapid progress. This is a similar pattern to the 'surges' of progress discussed in earlier case studies. This striking intensity suggests that once a vein of social communication is tapped into it seems to bubble to the surface very quickly.

The data for *eye contact* in Figure 10.4 show that incidence was negligible during the baseline phase. This increased steadily as soon as Intensive Interaction sessions started but only five weeks of intervention were possible before the end of term,

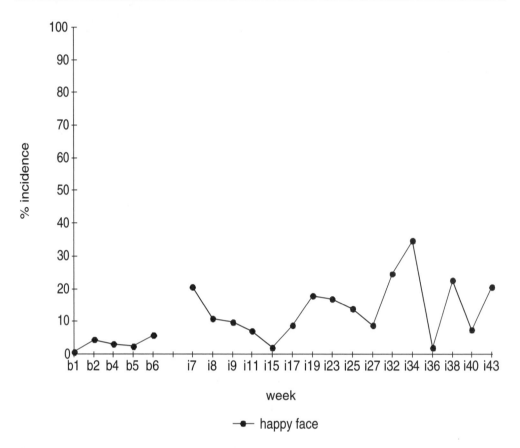

Figure 10.2 Percentage incidence of contingent happy/smiling face

which led to a four-week break before Intensive Interaction could be resumed. When Intensive Interaction sessions resumed *eye contact* incidence had regressed back to baseline levels but this did recover over a period of a few weeks. Interestingly the progress made with *eye contact* did not regress again with subsequent interruptions for school holidays. This suggests that a sustained uninterrupted period of intervention is necessary in the early stages of Intensive Interaction to cement any sociability progress and that progress is particularly vulnerable to regression in the early weeks when Intensive Interaction is just getting going. Similar patterns were also noticed in the other case studies and this has significant implications for optimum start-up times and for coordinators' organisational practice. Clearly it is preferable to begin Intensive Interaction with a pupil near the beginning rather than the middle or end of terms.

There was a marked surge in incidence of *joint focus* when Intensive Interaction was first introduced, followed by a similarly notable regression after the four-week break. Similar to the situation for *eye contact* discussed above, this regression did not

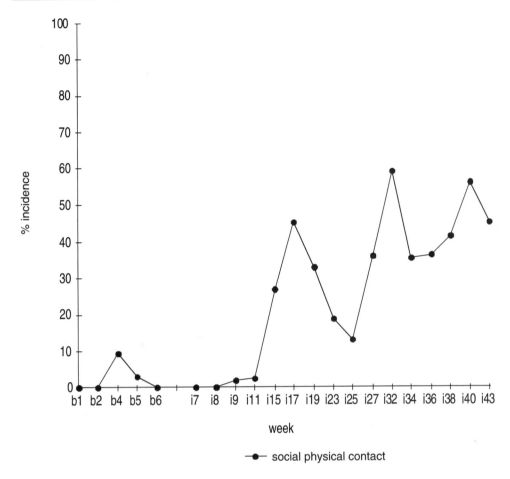

Figure 10.3 Percentage incidence of making/continuing/reciprocating social physical contact

occur to the same degree in subsequent holiday breaks. The average incidence of *joint focus* was 67 per cent in the intervention phase with two high peaks of 93 per cent and 94 per cent at weeks 25 and 43. In the final term of the project the average was 80 per cent. These are very high scores and show that Shane was able to concentrate and focus for sustained periods.

The data for *engagement* represent important evidence of sustained and absorbed social interaction and high levels of communication and sociability. Following the pattern that has been discussed for *eye contact* and *joint focus*, progress regressed following the fallow vacation period and then began to pick up again steadily once Intensive Interaction sessions resumed. The graph in Figure 10.6 shows a gradual build-up with occasional setbacks to a determinedly upward trend. The levels of progress made by Shane in the Intensive Interaction sessions were greater than any of the other five pupils in the study and yet where their progress was being

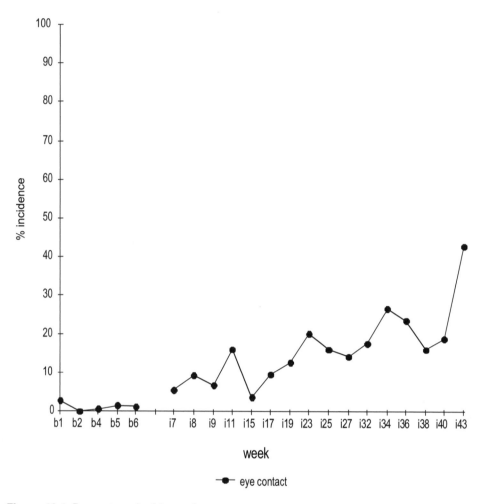

Figure 10.4 Percentage incidence for eye contact

transferred into the classroom Shane's was not. A closer look at data from typical classroom situations will help us probe a little deeper into this.

Very little progress was recorded in the typical classroom behaviour situations and the codes for 'head down' and 'sleepy/eyes closed' actually showed an increased incidence in the latter half of the project. This appears to support the theory that Shane was becoming bored and 'switching off'. The only behaviour code to show progress of any significance was that relating to Shane initiating contact with staff. Video evidence and interviews with Fleur and Jane depict a situation where Shane would go 'off task' and seek *eye contact* or *social physical contact* with one of the assistants. This led them to surmise that he was bored with the learning he was supposed to be engaged in (a teacher-led whole-class activity they felt he had progressed beyond). This of course can only ever be supposition, but the evidence of high levels of sus-

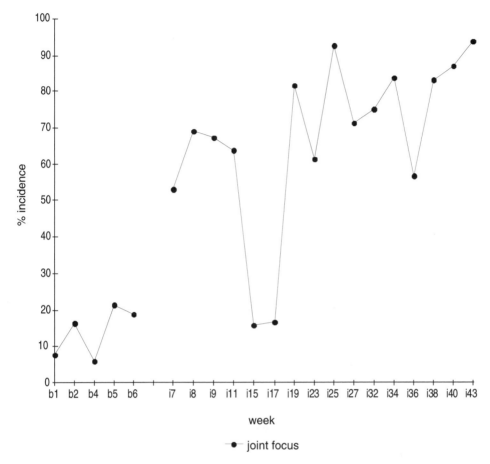

Figure 10.5 Percentage incidence of joint focus

tained *joint focus* in the Intensive Interaction sessions suggest that it was not necessarily an inability to stay on task that was the difficulty.

Other data that may shed some light on this is a comparison of the incidence of ritualistic chewing during Intensive Interaction and typical classroom situations (see Figure 10.7). In the Intensive Interaction sessions the ritualistic chewing all but disappeared. In typical classroom behaviour it showed an initial reduction but this was later followed by an increase. This increase coincides with the period of difficult micro-politics described earlier.

The data need to be analysed alongside important information from the historical log – the diary of other events across the duration of the project. The missing data point at week 11 relates to a zero incidence score when Shane's arm had been put in a splint to prevent him from using it to facilitate the ritualistic chewing. The lower incidence scores of weeks 38, 40 and 43 equate with a similar 'imposed' eradication strategy whereby Shane was required to hold a wooden bar in an attempt to

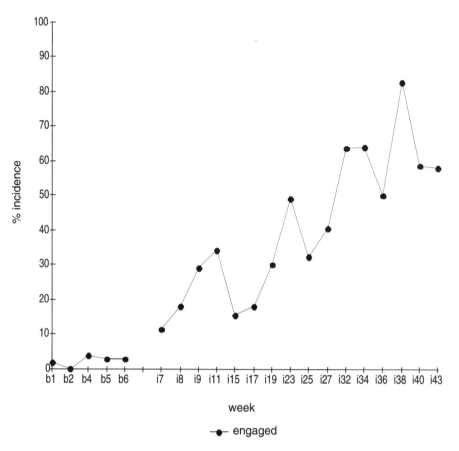

Figure 10.6 Percentage incidence of engagement

similarly prevent the chewing. This aspect of the case study raises several important questions. From a researcher's perspective – how does the data collector respond to practice she would not endorse? From the practitioner's perspective – why use artificial restraints/imposed mechanisms to prevent 'stereotyped' behaviour when the pupil can and does opt not to engage in it when we get the learning environment right for them? And from all of our perspectives – what can we learn from this about our attitudes and practice and about the role of such OSI/'stereotyped' behaviour for pupils? The fact that Shane's ritualistic chewing reduced to zero incidence during the Intensive Interaction sessions says much about the options for classroom strategies that support rather than oppress pupils (see Nind and Kellett 2002; Kellett 2003).

As the discussion of Shane's case study shows, classroom micro-politics can affect optimum levels of progress. Even if this is not visible during Intensive Interaction sessions it may well be apparent in a failure to transfer progress to other situations. The impact of micro-politics can be magnified or reduced with strong support from

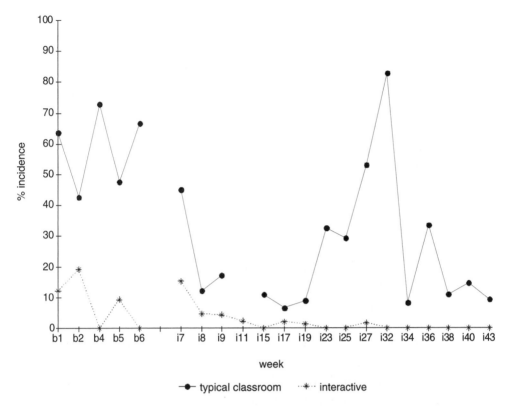

Figure 10.7 Comparative percentage incidences of 'ritualistic chewing' from typical classroom and interactive situations

senior management and the availability of an effective Intensive Interaction Coordinator. Neither of these conditions was present in Shane's situation which was, after all, just a school willing to be involved in a research project, not one committed to the approach.

Senior management support

If we are to learn from the experience of this project, then we must take away the message that if Intensive Interaction is going to be implemented with optimum outcomes then active support from senior management is essential. This needs to be at both an ideological and managerial level and at the earliest possible stage. A first step is involving senior management in Intensive Interaction workshops alongside staff who intend to practise. Ideally such training is best done as a whole-school exercise on a nominated training day, with senior managers visibly participating. Inviting the school governor with responsibility for inclusion to participate is a good way to raise the profile even more. Less ideally hands-on staff can attend training and feed back to colleagues and managers, but in this scenario the head teacher and others are already one step removed from the impetus and energy of the initiative. Innovation is best shared and followed up with clear lines of responsibility.

Senior managers can minimise some of the potentially damaging effects of class-room and staffroom micro-politics by resolving some of the issues that relate to Intensive Interaction at a pre-emptive stage. The following list outlines some of the positive actions that head teachers, curriculum managers and IINCOs can take to work towards a whole-school ethos and organisation which is supportive of good Intensive Interaction work.

- They can ensure that Intensive Interaction appears in curriculum planning documents and policy documents thereby offering some protection to what could be a vulnerable aspect of curriculum practice.
- They can give space in curriculum workshops and staff development seminars to follow up on initial training about the approach so that concerns and commitments are fully aired.
- They can give senior management 'weight' to legitimise daily time spent participating in Intensive Interaction thereby protecting the regularity of sessions.
- They can manage human resources so that team-working, including joint planning and reflection, is possible.
- They can participate in Intensive Interaction themselves, so they too have an investment in the approach and an understanding of the issues.

It is not uncommon for staff development sessions about Intensive Interaction to be dominated by discussion of how to deal with colleagues rather than how to access students. This tells us something about where the barriers to learning sometimes lie. Skilful practitioners can make good progress despite such barriers and in circumstances that are not at all conducive to good Intensive Interaction practice. They can, however, make better progress when they are fully supported and when attention is paid to the quality of the wider working, teaching and learning environment as well as to the quality of the interactions within it.

PART THREE

Best Practice

CHAPTER 11

Actively Seeking Optimum Progress

Introduction

The case for Intensive Interaction has already been made and there is a growing evidence base for its effectiveness in facilitating learners' progress. This book, though, is partly a response from the overwhelming feeling that we had in response to our last major study (Kellett 2001). We set out to evaluate the effectiveness of Intensive Interaction in children and soon found evidence of this effectiveness plus indications that, actually, the children could be making more progress. This led the study into how Intensive Interaction might be best implemented in schools and what we might do to facilitate optimum progress.

We have discussed the need to avoid complacency when we are involved in the pleasurable business of Intensive Interaction and the need for ongoing reflection both about the minutiae of practice and about the larger context. Our case studies highlight a whole range of factors that might impede or facilitate optimum progress. Here we take a more concentrated look at this critical issue, beginning with a discussion of the nature of progress for our pupils. We go on to look at how we measure pupils' progress and how we audit our own progress in bringing about good learning.

What is progress for participants in Intensive Interaction?

The need to think about what progress is for pupils involved in Intensive Interaction comes from a need to be clear about our concepts and also a need to challenge the imposed concepts coming from government standards agendas. We are acutely aware of the pressure felt by teachers and head teachers to achieve progress that is demonstrable on conventional assessments or even, preferably, formal measures such as national tests or SATs. We know some of the pressures in this, as one teacher commented:

Some children will be working towards level one for the whole of their school career, for them it does not provide a framework for progression in learning, they just fail.

(Garner *et al.* 1995: 68)

Nonetheless we can get sucked into competitive and norm-referenced thinking. The current wider context is the enterprise culture in which progress that is meaningful in the lives of our pupils often has no value in the marketplace, as school performance is judged by pupils' National Curriculum or 'p-level' performance (Aird 2001). There is also the danger of becoming preoccupied with the veneer of progress.

Inevitably, there are real tensions in all this. We clearly need some agreement about what we are aiming for so we can reach agreement about whether progress has occurred. The progress we are concerned with is educational – the kind of school progress that is usually measured in relation to the curriculum. The problem then emerges that if we have not sorted out the curriculum issues then we cannot begin to sort out the problem of what progress looks like. We already know that, for pupils with severe learning difficulties, demonstrating progress in relation to the National Curriculum, or the agreed curriculum framework outside England and Wales, is hugely problematic. The assessment framework that comes with this curriculum is far too crude for the sort of progress with which we are concerned. There are also issues of relevance. If we are looking for progress in autonomy, quality of life, ability to form relationships and so on, then we have to be explicit that this is our curriculum. If we want the kinds of progress that Intensive Interaction can bring about, we have to engage with this and not an alternative, normative agenda.

Teachers who have been involved with further education during the last decade will also be very familiar with the concept of whether progress has to be linear or whether it can be horizontal. The 'schedule 2' fiasco brought this into sharp profile. This came from the Further Education Funding Council specification that funding would only be available for courses leading to qualifications or to courses on this hierarchy. Teachers everywhere felt that their students with learning difficulties were making progress within their courses such that they could continue them meaningfully, or even start new courses at the 'same level' but with different challenges. This, however, did not match the official concept of progress as linear – moving up some ladder of steps, rather than horizontal – moving out to new areas. This schedule led to much opposition and is now gone. Back in 1996 SCAA recognised the problem of providing evidence of progress and did some reconceptualising of it in their document *Assessment, Recording and Accreditation of Achievement for Pupils with Learning Difficulties*. What they retained, however, was a hierarchical framework of expectation.

With our target pupil-group in mind, Ouvry and Saunders (1996) made the case for a more lateral concept of progress related to pupils' ability to understand, interact with and control the environment, develop and extend existing skills, retain or reactivate skills and accept reduced support in completing a task. This horizontal or lateral dimension to progress is recognised by the QCA who state: 'For pupils with learning difficulties, progression is not necessarily only movement up a hierarchical ladder of skills and knowledge. Lateral progression is also important' (QCA 2001a: 14). Lateral progression is very familiar to us in Intensive Interaction. We put effort into supporting pupils to widen their repertoire of interactive games and to engage them in new contexts and with new people. We see it as progress when pupils use their growing skills in new ways and when they use them spontaneously.

This does not mean that there is not a vertical dimension to progress in Intensive Interaction. There is one, it is just that it is not all-encompassing. We look for pupils to move from being passive or rejecting of interactions, to enjoying them, actively participating in them, anticipating and taking risks, and ultimately initiating interactions. In recognising progress we look for interactions that are longer, have more variations, and involve increased engagement (Hewett and Nind 1998; Nind and Hewett 2001).

The concept of progress in Intensive Interaction also has a holistic dimension. We are less interested in pupils achieving skills that are part of an official hierarchy or part of a subset needed to perform a particular task. We are more concerned with facilitating abilities that enhance the pupils' quality of life and quality of relationships with others. These are abilities that we see emerging in context and that cannot be measured out of context. They happen in relation to each other.

Our concept of progress is not just holistic but also, crucially, dynamic. Central to our understanding of Intensive Interaction is that it is accumulative. It gathers its own momentum as making progress in one area almost always leads to progress in other areas. When pupils are better able to reward others for spending time with them, they tend to get more and better quality interactions in which they learn new abilities to sustain interactions, which in turn become more sophisticated and so on. When we actively seek progress through Intensive Interaction we do not systematically work our way through a hierarchical checklist of skills, but rather explore a network of interconnected abilities with all kinds of inbuilt possibilities. This does not, we must add, assume that we embark on this exploration without a map. We are in some senses working our way towards some end-point of good social, communicative and cognitive abilities supported with good emotional well-being, through a very well established route. This is the route of 'normal' development within the context of nurturing interactions. We are reminded of the story of the man asking for directions to Milton Keynes, and the helpful person to whom the request for directions was made answering, 'Well, you don't want to start from here.' Our route starts very much from where the child is. There are also some markers along the way to indicate that we have not got lost (such as the development of contingent vocalisation or the onset of initiation of social contact). But with this route and map there are lots of possibilities. This is a concept of a journey and progress without the usual rigidities that close us down.

A further element in the concept of progress we are arguing for here concerns the importance of the minutiae. Ware and Healey (1994: 13) summed up that 'progress is to some extent in the eye of the beholder' and some of what we are advocating is educating the eye to see better. We have to be willing to look for progress that can be easily missed but that is nonetheless incredibly significant. Evidence of learning for pupils with severe or complex learning difficulties is often obscured by the very limited nature of individuals' behavioural repertoires and by their medical conditions such as epilepsy (Barber and Goldbart 1998). Barriers to seeing progress also come from our sometimes unsophisticated outlook and crude measures. We often tell the story of Selma Fraiberg's (1974) study, in which she was able to help mothers of blind children to see how their babies were responding to their interactive efforts in their arm and hand movements. Previously, the mothers had sought and failed to find evidence of this because they limited their looking to their children's faces. They had to be helped to see what was there and so do we in our classroom interactions. The more meaningful the context is, the more likely we are to see progress and the more skilled we become at knowing what we are looking for and how to look.

In *A Practical Guide to Intensive Interaction* (Nind and Hewett 2001) we write about 'moving on' in a way that gives a framework for bringing about and recognising progress that focuses on what we as practitioners do as much as what the learners do. Thus, our concept of progress is one that is mutual. In Intensive Interaction terms, progress is as much about moving on in respect of how we respond, in our interpretations and in the experiences we offer, as about what the pupil learns to do. We return to this theme in the next section.

How can we measure progress?

In special education we have a history of checklists measuring progress against developmental steps or individual targets. Checklists can even be made to relate to the curriculum. As Ware and Healey (1994) have ably argued though, checklists are problematic because the selection and ordering of items is contentious and sensitivity to small progress is hard to achieve. Checklists match with a more hierarchical, less dynamic concept of progress than the one we are advocating. An important lesson in the early days of Intensive Interaction was that we could not use old checklist or ticklist-style measures to assess and record progress in complex, dynamic interactions. There was quite simply poor fitness for purpose.

In looking for an alternative, some infant developmental indices can be helpful as these link well with what we are trying to teach and they can be sensitive enough to discern small progress. Their linearity, however, can still be unhelpfully rigid and not take into account the different life experiences and circumstances of pupils with SLD and PMLD.

Another alternative is Vygotskian approaches, which acknowledge that learning is interpersonal. Measuring progress from this perspective points us to looking not just at what a pupil can achieve alone, but at what they can achieve with the assistance of a more skilled person. This is very pertinent for the content of Intensive Interaction. Notions of independent achievement are nonsensical when we are concerned with communication and sociability. None of us can do these alone – by their very nature they concern abilities that we demonstrate with others. Inevitably, how skilled our interactive partners are makes a difference to how skilled we are – and this is crucial to achieving and measuring progress in Intensive Interaction.

Observational approaches suit this concern with looking at communication and social abilities in the context of interactions. The data collected for the case studies in this book largely came through systematic observation and video analysis. This approach is usually associated with behavioural techniques and is borrowed from experimental research. What is different for us, though, is that we are interested in the dimension of the other interactive partner. We have measures of the progress Jacob and Sam and the other children made *with* their interactive partners. They jointly own the progress. If we could enhance the practice of the teacher-partner then we could enhance the progress of the pupil-partner. This is not cheating. It is seeing learning in context and recognising that we are all interdependent. With pupils with PMLD what they can achieve with us, rather than what they can achieve without us, is our prime concern. Systematic observation can be very time-consuming and requires skilled observers, but it does offer great fitness for our purpose, particularly with regard to the need to see the minutiae of progress.

Also appropriate to the horizontal, dynamic and particularly holistic dimensions of progress are the narrative approaches that evolved alongside Intensive Interaction. Most well known are the strategies of writing a narrative account of interactions immediately after they have happened and of focusing these somewhat on the questions of: what happened, what was significant and how did it feel? (Nind and Hewett 2001). These narrative strategies facilitate reflection on the important but much-maligned subjective, as well as observable, elements of progress.

Doing Intensive Interaction and doing it as well as we can

Doing what we can to actively seek optimum progress requires us to understand what we mean by progress and to have a means of recognising and recording it when it happens. We also need to do the things that are discussed in this book as a whole. We need to keep faithful to the key principles of Intensive Interaction, so that what we are offering pupils is that which is based on lessons from developmental psychology and that which has been shown to be effective. It is all too easy to pick on elements of Intensive Interaction that seem most doable, and offer these in a weak imitation of the approach (see discussions in Nind 2000; Nind *et al.* 2001; and Nind and Kellett 2002). These imitations may facilitate progress, but not the best possible progress.

Furthermore, we need to attend to the implementation of the approach, so that practitioners are empowered to do their best in the best possible circumstances. The case studies are full of lessons about how the approach can be enhanced, or undermined, by factors in the real and imperfect world in which we operate. We cannot always achieve optimum conditions for doing Intensive Interaction, but it helps enormously to at least know what they are. Equally, research about the minimum standard of training and number and quality of sessions adds to our knowledge base about what works in Intensive Interaction in different contexts (Samuel 2001).

Auditing Intensive Interaction

One way of focusing on actively seeking progress in pupils is to audit our own progress as professionals in providing a coherent Intensive Interaction approach within the curriculum. This was an idea that emerged from an action research project in one London borough in which the advisory service and newly established Intensive Interaction Coordinators wanted to be able to evaluate the progress the schools were making. The Audit Framework, which we outline in Boxes 11.1 to 11.3, is currently being piloted in schools and colleges. The Framework attempts to set out dimensions of what is going on when Intensive Interaction is emerging as an approach in a school, when it is established and when there is advanced competence and commitment, such that the school can act as a training resource for others. The emerging/established/advanced stages are applied across three dimensions: the practitioners' interactive style and individual practice; whole-school issues; and long-term issues.

We begin with the individual practitioner (see Box 11.1), where the Framework draws on all our experience of the stages we go through in becoming a skilled interactive partner using Intensive Interaction to the full. The Framework also incorporates our concern with our verbal as well as broader interactive style (Nind *et al.* 2001). Thus it incorporates skilled use of motherese, the style of verbal interaction found to be valuable in supporting infants' progress towards verbal communication (Weistuch and Byers-Brown 1987).

The second Framework in Box 11.2 goes beyond the individual practitioner to address the school-based issues.

The final Framework being piloted (see Box 11.3) concerns this issue of main-

Interactive style and practice of Intensive Interaction		
Emerging	**Established**	**Advanced**
Practitioners engage in lots of 'doing to' pupils – offering stimuli, and are beginning to observe and build on responses.	'Doing to' pupils is balanced by 'doing with', observation is sensitive and responsiveness is established practice.	The limitations of 'doing to' are fully recognised. Practitioners are comfortable with seeking participation rather than compliance. Observation is skilful, sensitive and critical.
Practitioners use basic imitation in interactions.	Practitioners make skilful use of selective imitation.	Practitioners use turnarounds. Practitioners make skilful use of the nurturing interactive style, including motherese, employed to facilitate progress in cognitive, emotional, social and communicative development.
Practitioners use playfulness, physical contact, adjusted interpersonal behaviour, rhythm and timing to attract and hold attention.	Practitioners make skilful use of the nurturing interactive style to create anticipation, turn-taking and engagement.	
Practitioners adapt their verbal style to attract and hold attention.	Practitioners make skilful use of motherese to provide commentaries on joint activity and to infer communicative intent.	
Practitioners are willing to adapt their interactive style based on observing others and knowing the principles.	Practitioners' interactive style evolves with adaptations based on observing others, knowing the principles, and reflecting on these and their own experiences.	Practitioners are critically aware of their own developing interactive style and engage in regular self-appraisal.
Practitioners are able to access pupils who are easier to reach and interactive games are developing.	Practitioners are able to establish repertoires of interactive games with pupils who are easier to reach.	The repertories of interactive games are varied in content and intensity.
	Access and interactive game is achieved with pupils who are difficult to reach.	The most challenging, least rewarding pupils are accessed and interactive games are developing.
	Difficult patches for pupils are handled confidently, using Intensive Interaction to maintain a relationship.	Pupils' expressions of complex and negative as well as positive emotions are handled confidently, using critical reflection on Intensive Interaction and other strategies and boundaries.

Box 11.1 Framework for interactive style and practice

Whole-school issues		
Emerging	**Established**	**Advanced**
Interest in Intensive Interaction (II) is established in the school and being turned into action in places.	Interest in II is pervasive and being turned into action across a range of classes.	Interest in II is established and acted upon wherever relevant.
Some staff still need encouragement to get involved in II.	The extent to which the school is adopting the approach has been discussed and resolved.	There is whole-school commitment to II which is incorporated within whole-school policies.
There is much trial and error as staff 'have a go'.	Experimentation becomes more systematic with emerging ideas about what works.	There is ongoing reflection on the process of II.
Good, intuitive interactive work among colleagues is recognised and valued.	Staff are comfortable with II both as intuitive and planned work.	Interactivity (intuitive style and using incidental opportunities) and regular, planned and recorded II sessions are incorporated into the life of the school.
II occurs in specific sessions, e.g. soft play, drama, PSHE, and aims for interaction are incorporated into lesson planning.	General lesson and individual planning reflects a concern with interactive aims and processes.	A wide range of lessons are designed to maximise the quality of interactions and learning through interactive processes.
Written work on II is emerging in an ad hoc way.	There is sharing of paperwork concerned with planning and recording.	There is a written policy on II and safe practice guidelines, either as separate documents or as integral to other policies.
Proponents of II emerge.	There is whole-staff involvement with II at some level.	There is whole-school coordination of II. A coordinator is responsible for staff development on II, policy, information for parents, building towards a collaborative culture, sharing good practice and maintaining momentum.

Box 11.2 Framework for whole-school issues

taining momentum and good practice in the long term which requires an optimum climate echoing aspects of the learning organisation described by Wenger (1998).

Feedback on this approach to auditing indicates that it helps to avoid complacency. We can map whether as an individual or a school we are sitting comfortably or making inroads, whether we have gone as far as we can for the time being or as far as we want to. Inevitably, when groups of individuals set about mapping where they and their establishment are, there is heated discussion and the profile is rarely neat. We can be advanced in some areas and barely begun in others. But we are at least pointed to good starting points and places to aim for so that we, as well as our pupils, make progress.

Establishing a climate, keeping up momentum and monitoring developments		
Emerging	Established	Advanced
There are the beginnings of thinking about and recording interactions – mainly at a descriptive level.	Thinking about and recording of interactions are reflective and analytical.	The meta-level – practitioners' reflections on interaction are further reflected upon.
A language to describe interactive practice and principles in school begins to emerge.	A common language is developed to articulate the interactive work staff are engaged with.	There is regular critical dialogue with colleagues and parents.
Time is given to discussing the aims of II and to sharing aspects of practice.	Regular time for discussion and dissemination is embedded in the school day/week/year.	There is ongoing staff development to enhance practice and enable troubleshooting.
		Advanced practitioners are able to support the introduction of II outside school, e.g. in homes, other schools, college.
There is a climate of openness to trying II.	Opportunities are created for staff to work with like-minded colleagues to enhance understanding and practice of II. There is no pressure to perform but an obligation to enable.	Opportunities are created for collaborative work, apprenticeship-style support of new staff, and problem-solving partnerships for difficult issues or pupils who are hard to reach.
		Use of II in school is audited.
		There is critical awareness of interface between II and other approaches.
		There is critical awareness of accountability issues: the need for continuity, progression, written and video records, dialogue with parents and advocates and safe practice guidelines.

Box 11.3 Framework for maintaining momentum

CHAPTER 12

The Curriculum

Teachers who 'do' Intensive Interaction in schools in England and Wales inevitably also 'do' the National Curriculum. How they put the two together, however, varies considerably. Combining them is a source of much anxiety and much creativity. It is something that we are asked about often. Our response here is not to give a directive answer about how Intensive Interaction and the National Curriculum are best put together. This book is intended to support and guide and give ideas, but not to be prescriptive. Instead we air some of the issues, debate some of the options and ultimately make a case for the place of Intensive Interaction in the curriculum. Readers outside England and Wales may be tempted to skip this chapter, but there are wider curriculum issues that will be of interest to readers without the National Curriculum.

We begin by putting the National Curriculum in context. The National Curriculum (NC) is not *the* curriculum. It is not the whole into which everything we do in school must be subsumed. *Curriculum Guidance 3: The Whole Curriculum* (NCC 1990) stated 'the NC alone will not provide the necessary breadth'; the whole curriculum includes the NC subjects and 'an accepted range of cross-curricular elements' and extra-curricular activities. Also stressed in this government guidance are the intangibles of the spirit and ethos of school and its teaching methods: 'The ERA does not prescribe how pupils should be taught' – this remains teachers' remit. This important truth has often been forgotten or eroded, however, and must, in our view, be reclaimed.

The National Curriculum Council has been keen to stress the importance of the place of the NC alongside other curricular elements for pupils with SLD/PMLD in particular. Their 1992 advice was that for these pupils the NC alone would not be able to meet *all* their needs; it was intended to build on and supplement, not replace, specialist curricula. SCAA (1996) reinforced this need to divide time between the NC and additional curricula responding to pupil need. This was again stressed in the 1994 Dearing Report when the slimming down of the NC to 80 per cent of school time allowed greater time for teaching skills, therapies and alternative curricula. Unfortunately, this common-sense approach has not always been evident in Ofsted inspections.

We know, of course, that concern with skills teaching and therapies came later as an afterthought. Ware's (1994: 62) discussion of this issue makes plain that many of the challenges arise because 'the construction of the NC did not address the potential tension of designing a curriculum for all while taking account of the diversity of pupils'. So what are the tensions? They are:

- the hope of curricular inclusion versus the spectre of exclusion;
- joining in because it is for everyone versus questioning whether it is helpful for anyone;
- previous notions of good curricular practice versus the NC;
- balance and breadth on one hand and differentiation and relevance on the other;
- what society needs and what individuals need;
- being in the mainstream or having a curriculum below level 1;
- how much to push the flexibility of the NC;
- how much to pay lip service to the NC;
- entitlement to access but access to what?

We need to bear these tensions (and opportunities) in mind as we review the options available to us.

Options for managing the NC and other curricula

Some of the options for managing the NC and other curricula have been outlined by Ware (1994):

1. To have a pre-NC curriculum, for those not yet at NC level, e.g. a developmental curriculum. But would this be seen as a separate and second-best curriculum, effectively a form of exclusion?
2. To uncouple assessment in the key stages from chronological age. This would take out some of the inbuilt failure, but it would go against the fashion for age-appropriateness.
3. To modify the statements of attainment and so offer a modified NC.
4. To assess a broader range of activities. This would bring in concepts of horizontal progress across a level.
5. To have more refined assessment arrangements, e.g. assessing how much help was given to attain assessment targets.

All of these options set the pupils apart in some way from the central concept of a curriculum for all. The range of options we can consider, however, goes further than Ware's early list and includes:

6. Aird's (2001) idea of a core curriculum with personal learning styles at the centre, with specialist curricula covering management of mobility, sensory and perceptual education, independent living skills and emotional, behavioural and social education, but also conventional subjects: maths, English and communication and ICT. These conventional subjects are chosen based on educational processes of enabling, engaging, empowering and equipping. Other subjects form a peripheral curriculum.

As more options unfold, issues of principle emerge: How important is it to be seen as the same as other pupils? How much is the problem with the NC subjects and how much with the assessment framework? How important is it that we are honest about what we are doing?

Grove and Peacey (1999) add three more options, based on a simple analysis of the three most basic choices:

7. To provide the NC plus complementary curricula. The problem with this, they recognise, is that the curriculum gets fragmented and overcrowded. Some schools have gone for making the most relevance they can from the NC but prioritising resources and energies for the remaining 20 per cent of school time for other curricula. This kind of strategy has been undermined by the temptation of directing resources at the National Literacy Strategy and National Numeracy Strategy.
8. To redescribe pre-NC curriculum practice in NC terms, e.g., calling Intensive Interaction English or science. Byers (1999) has warned against the folly of this curriculum as an elaborate pretence and SCAA (1996) state that tokenism should not be tolerated.
9. To use NC subjects as 'contexts of experience' in which pupils are able to follow their own goals alongside others following NC goals. Thus their curriculum would still be relevant, and even enriched and more stimulating, and they would not be isolated. Pupils are less learning *about* the subject than learning *through* the subject (Ouvry and Saunders 1996).

Byers (1999) argues teachers have mostly rejected 7 and 8 in favour of 9 and furthermore that teachers are skilful at this and make it meaningful. In an action research project with a special school whose changing populations presented a real challenge for the curriculum we (Nind and Cochrane 2002) devised something similar – our next option:

10. Teachers think of the curriculum in terms of processes rather than content. Within this they identify subject-related processes; learning to learn processes; and general processes (see Figure 12.1). This provides a bank of processes for lesson planning and different pupils can have different emphases. This is not unlike Sebba *et al.*'s (1995) 'mapping individual learning routes' through

'meaningful, relevant group activity'. There can be fluidity here so that a pupil is not always a 'pre-NC' pupil; there are no dividing lines to categorise pupils by deterministic ideas of ability (Hart in press). Intensive Interaction is primarily about learning to learn processes, and this is not lost in this framework (Box 12.1), even though acknowledgement is made of the links with subjects and the skills pupils need to rehearse on a daily basis.

11. The QCA preparatory or 'p'-level approaches similarly mix the generic and the domain-specific, but rather than focusing on process, these offer a 'jumble of developmental/behaviourist/academic strategies' (Aird 2001: 6). Despite the problem of creating a hierarchy when there is a need for much lateral progression, the curriculum framework associated with p-levels fits the tradition of small incremental steps. A p-level curriculum is a government-endorsed version of Ware's first option (number 1 of our list). Many of the abilities rehearsed and developed in Intensive Interaction would be recognised among the stages.

Figures 12.1 to 12.4 summarise some of these options in a way that teachers may find helpful for their decision-making.

The issue of rights and entitlements

Much of the rhetoric around the NC is rhetoric about the 'entitlement' to 'access' this curriculum. Curriculum Guidance Nine suggested access for pupils with SLD/PMLD through subject-led activities, other subjects, cross-curricular themes and incidental teaching. The QCA Curriculum Guidelines for Pupils Attaining Significantly Below Age-Related Expectations similarly offers strategies for accessing the NC.

For some educationalists however, this concept of entitlement to the NC has led to broader questions of entitlement. Norwich (1990: 159–60) argues that entitlements can be 'double-edged, particularly if the entitlement is to something which is not relevant to the needs of particular children. In such cases entitlements can turn into rigid impositions.' Aird (2001: 44) maintains that yes, pupils have a right to access the NC, but actually they have more urgent and important rights. One of the teachers in Potter and Whittaker's (2001: 160) study of children with autism has a clear position on this:

> Is it not a more basic right to learn to communicate . . . to learn to interact? And if that takes three-quarters of the time given for the curriculum then I feel that's important and it should not be balanced – it should be teaching the skills the children need.

Clearly then, the right to a broad and balanced curriculum can come into conflict with the right to learn early skills. There can be tension between apparent curricular

Subject-related processes	Learning to learn processes	General processes
Related to scientific, mathematical, musical etc. domains.	Related to empowering the learner for further learning – not domain-specific.	The kinds of processes we need to rehearse on a daily basis in school, but which need not necessarily lead us into further learning or be related to subject domains.
e.g. Scientific: • Sorting • Classifying • Testing • Observing • Comparing Mathematical • Counting • Measuring • Sequencing Musical • Rhythm • Tempo • Responding to pitch	e.g. • attending • collaborating • interpreting others' thoughts and feelings • exploring • trying out • remembering • anticipating • enjoying together	e.g. • choosing • listening • watching • manipulating • writing • waiting

The framework was prompted by observing a science lesson in which the pupils did not do anything related to science concepts but a lot of conforming to school rules and rehearsing the skills they had been involved with all morning.

Many processes could appear in more than one category. The important part is thinking about the meaningfulness of the lesson for the individual and group.

A lesson plan e.g. science: materials and their properties with a wet and dry goods stimulus could involve the following processes: observing, comparing, sorting, predicting, exploring, manipulating, communicating preferences, joint focus, turn-taking, sharing proximity... These would be available to all and targeted for some. Significantly, whether the focus is on subject processes or individual learning to learn priorities, the learning is embedded rather than added on.

Useful resources for this type of planning are:

• Sebba, J., Byers, R. and Rose, R. (1995) *Redefining the Whole Curriculum for Pupils with Learning Difficulties* (2nd edn). London: David Fulton.

• Babbage, R., Byers, R. and Redding, H. (1999) *Approaches to Teaching and Learning: Including Pupils with Learning Difficulties*. London: David Fulton.

• Davis, J. (2001) *A Sensory Approach to the Curriculum for Pupils with Profound and Multiple Learning Difficulties*. London: David Fulton.

Box 12.1 Framework for option 10 process approach

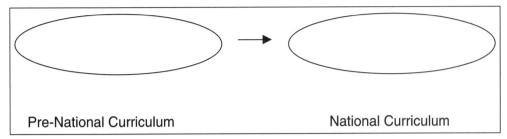

Figure 12.1 Sequential: options 1 and 11

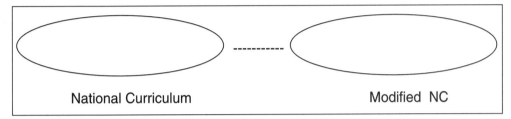

Figure 12.2 Parallel: option 3

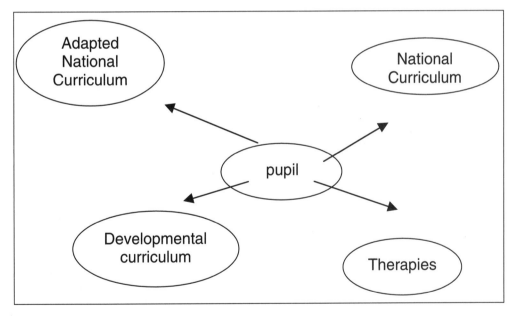

Figure 12.3 Fragmented: option 7

Developmental curriculum

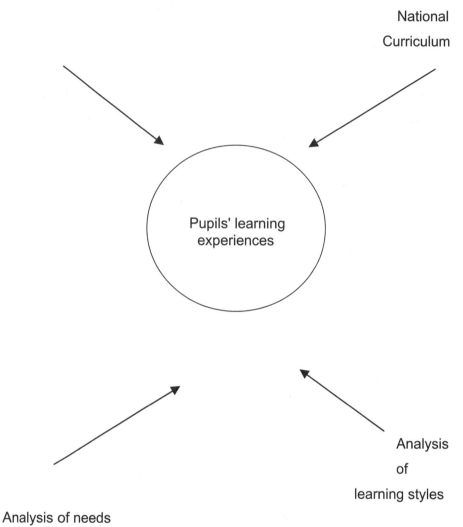

Figure 12.4 Experiential/process-led: options 9 and 10

inclusion and more fundamental social inclusion. Cornell and Garden (1990) argue that where there is incompatibility, the special school curriculum should win as it is specially designed with pupils' needs in mind. This may be a somewhat simplistic solution to a complex problem. As Byers and Rose (1994) and Carpenter *et al.* (1996) have argued before us, we would maintain that we need to exert some control over the curriculum in the face of external pressures. We need to retain our evaluative skills when we make educational judgements. Aird (2001) criticises the readiness with which teachers have focused energies on the challenge of engaging pupils with SLD/PMLD in the NC in a meaningful way rather than questioning the relevance of the curriculum itself. He cites SCAA's (1997) finding that 34 per cent of teachers in SLD schools disagreed that the NC offered a proper basis for a curriculum relevant to their pupils; yet still they search for access and endless differentiation. For Aird, it is the threat of failing Ofsted that has made schools fall in line and invest in the NC as a priority. For us, there is also something more about the lure of being a part of the mainstream, talking the same talk as other teachers, while retaining a sense of the special, and perhaps a healthy readiness to question the sanctity of the old skills-based curriculum.

Learning from early years curricula

The issue of entitlement is a useful one. What are and should our pupils be entitled to? What is it that we are really trying to achieve and how can we achieve it? As Nind (2002) has argued elsewhere, we have much to learn from early years educators. Kelly (1994), for example, is clear that the early years curriculum must be developmentally appropriate, that is, based on children's development and interests and not on traditional subjects or knowledge acquisition. It must be child-centred and based on all the language, communication and stimuli around children, and on an understanding of how children learn in the early stages.

Blenkin (1994) shares this clarity: the curriculum should nurture the child's development; it should be seen in terms of processes rather than content – these are interlinked and should be planned holistically. Blenkin and Kelly (1993: 58) argue that 'a curriculum divided into subjects is, potentially, the most alienating form of curriculum for young children because it formalises experience too soon and, in doing so, makes it distant from the everyday, common sense knowledge and learning that the child is familiar with and responsive to'. Blenkin and Kelly are not atypical. The whole early years literature is against over-formalisation of the curriculum at this stage because of the adverse effects it has on children's learning (Pugh 1996).

Early years educators feel on safe ground here. They do not have the history of exclusion that surrounds pupils with SLD/PMLD and, therefore, not the need to buy into and be a part of the NC (Nind 2002). It may be easier when you know this different curriculum is for one part of a child's school career and not for the long term. Nonetheless, we urge teachers of children with SLD to share some of this focus on the need to provide an optimum learning environment for where children are now in their development, so that they might establish firm foundations for all their later learning. The QCA's (1999) Early Learning Goals are about 'laying secure foundations for later learning' – why is this so different for us? We can learn from early years practitioners' readiness to value three-year-olds as three-year-olds and not four-or five-year-olds in the making. We can share their starting point of what the child can do rather than what he/she cannot do; and their view of adults as enablers (Lloyd 1997). We can even learn about how to plan our curriculum in keeping with this philosophy. At Pen Green, for example, teachers developed a versatile curriculum planning framework – the PLOD chart: Possible Lines of Direction – which allows for pursuing class themes and individual children's burning interests (Whalley 1994). Many early years educators feel they have moved towards the NC without sacrificing their child-centred nursery tradition (Sylva *et al.* 1992). Perhaps if we start from such a strong principled position based on good pedagogy we can achieve this too.

Getting off the hamster wheel

Our impression is that for many teachers going back to a strong principled position based on good pedagogy first requires getting off the hamster wheel. By this we mean the trap of endlessly going forward (or round in circles), seeking new ways of accessing the curriculum and ever-more complex differentiation. Reinforcement from Ofsted inspectors can make this feel like safe territory and to get off is to take a risk. To get off is also to reclaim lost responsibility for bigger decisions about the curriculum. For newer teachers, this is responsibility they have never enjoyed and understandably dangerous territory for them. There is something quite fundamental about giving yourself permission to work from your own sense of integrity as a teacher and to move out from very narrow parameters.

If the hamster wheel feels comfortable we can recite all the government paperwork and 'rules' that say this is the only way it can be done. If we want to get off, however, we can find plenty of government paperwork and 'rules' to endorse our choice. We might feel uncomfortable with Aird's (2001: 14) idea of specialist curricula far removed from the NC, but more comfortable with the Early Learning Goals (QCA 1999) and the idea of good teaching and learning for all (at that stage of development). We might feel uneasy about rejecting teaching 'subjects' but good about adopting the QCA (2001a: 27) framework of encounter; awareness; attention and response; engagement; participation; involvement; and gaining skills and understanding. There is nothing to fear, in terms of Intensive Interaction finding a place in the curriculum, from SCAA's (1996: 11–13) key principles:

- Planning begins with pupil's needs, interests, aptitudes and achievements.
- Pupils are entitled to a broad and balanced curriculum, including the NC ('this principle recognises that legal entitlement is only meaningful if the pupil is actively participating rather than simply being present', p. 11).
- Pupils have access to programmes of study that enable them to progress and demonstrate achievement.
- Teachers distinguish between achievement in planning, assessing, teaching, recording and reporting.

- Curriculum provides progression and continuity.
- Planning takes account of issues (such as communication) which permeate the whole curriculum.
- Planning is subject-focused, but recognises links between subjects.

There is plenty of official documentation that endorses Intensive Interaction in the curriculum. For example the QCA's (2001b) *Planning, teaching and assessing the curriculum for pupils with learning difficulties: Developing Skills* cites Intensive Interaction as an example of a specific teaching approach that pupils may need (p. 5). Similarly, their General Guidelines (QCA 2001a: 16) cite it as a 'therapeutic treatment' which might form part of individual support programmes for some pupils. While we would not sideline the approach in this way, it is an endorsement if we want one. We may need this kind of permission to provide an optimum learning environment or we may feel secure enough in our own professionalism to not need such permission. Either way, it is possible to get off the hamster wheel. It is an achievable goal to manage the NC and Intensive Interaction in a way that offers a curriculum that has real integrity.

CHAPTER 13

Intensive Interaction and Accountability

Accountability for Intensive Interaction is not a new concern. In the early exploratory stage in which Intensive Interaction was developed staff were conscious of this issue. The 1980s were a different era in terms of the pressures for accountability, and in the hospital setting accountability to parents took on a very different feel from today's efforts for increased partnership with parents and their new roles as active consumers of education. Nonetheless, we were acutely aware of our accountability – to our students, primarily, but also to managers, parents, employers and governors. In *Access to Communication* (Nind and Hewett 1994) we stressed the need to show that Intensive Interaction was much more than 'having a good time'. This reflected the contrast for us from highly structured work offering the security of prescribed objectives and tick-list records, and perhaps also some guilt at the pleasure we felt in working in this way.

In this chapter we address accountability in the twenty-first century and within the school context in particular. We address the challenge of developing appropriate school and classroom systems for planning, recording, developing policy, sharing aspirations and results, and facing inspection by Ofsted. Because it is often at the forefront of teachers' minds, we begin with the last first.

Ofsted

We hear a lot of anecdotal accounts about Ofsted and even more about people's anxieties than about their experiences. Our attempts to get to the heart of the problem take us to the issue of Intensive Interaction being about processes and interactions and not about products and objectives.

> One of the main differences between behavioural and 'interactive/process' approaches . . . is the sense of what we might call 'linearity' endowed by behavioural approaches and not necessarily gained from interactive/process approaches.

By this we mean the reassuring sensation that the teacher is attempting to set out the teaching in small, sequential, easily controlled steps, with one step logically following on from the other. Each step has its own target and any teaching session is coherently related to the whole because of the presence of a session target. The learning attainments can be observed and measured similarly. The reassurance comes primarily from the sense of control over the learning that the teacher is able to observe and exert, from the sense of an accurate diagnosis of what is still to be learnt. This can give a (perhaps false) impression that involving the learner with the tasks is purposeful. Reassurance comes also from the ease with which assessment and record-keeping can demonstrate the overall sense of control to others, such as Ofsted inspectors.

(Hewett and Nind 1998: 282–3)

In contrast to objectives-led approaches, Intensive Interaction offers none of these reassurances to teachers or Ofsted inspectors and so we have to look for other sources of security with what we are doing.

We can use some old-fashioned task analysis-type skills to help us to understand what is involved here:

- the need to show clarity of thinking about our purpose and methods;
- the need to show planning in our teaching;
- the need to show familiarity with, and observation of, preordained curricular expectations;
- the need to show adequate systems for monitoring progress;
- the need to show that progress is indeed happening.

All of these challenges are easier with a simplistic, linear model of learning, but we can meet them perfectly well, if with more effort and creativity, with a more naturalistic model of learning. We address them in turn.

Clarity

Any lack of clarity on our part is likely to become an issue at inspection. However, we know that schools where there is a real commitment to Intensive Interaction, and where staff communicate this clearly in their documentation rather than apologise for it, have received positive feedback. On the plus side, inspectors are asked to judge 'how well the school provides for *all* its pupils' (Ofsted 1996/97: 3) and some schools have successfully highlighted their Intensive Interaction work as an important part of their approach to providing for pupils with the most extreme difficulties. On a less positive note we also know that Ofsted use a lot of mainstream models and many teams do not follow NCC/SCAA/QCA advice about the balance between NC and other curricula (Aird 2001), which means they devalue other curricula in their appraisal. While we cannot make QCA and Ofsted communicate better and operate more coherently, it may pay to make reference to these guidelines explicit. For example, we can cite the QCA's (2001b: 4) *Developing Skills* guidelines on *Planning, teaching and assessing the curriculum for pupils with learning difficulties*, which states:

> For pupils with learning difficulties, the key skill of communication is fundamental to participation and achievement in all curriculum areas.

And that this includes:

- responding to others, for example, through facial expression or gestures;
- communicating with others, for example, expressing preferences and needs;
- interacting with others, for example, through mutual gaze with another or joint participation (p. 4);
- perhaps needing 'specific teaching approaches' such as 'intensive interaction' (p. 5).

Planning

Later in the chapter we offer more practical advice on planning, but first we discuss the need to present our work at its best. We know that inspectors look at how the school provides for different groups; values them; monitors their progress; how well particular groups are taught; and how well the school cares for its pupils. We also know that we need to provide them with sources of evidence – to spell it out for them. This was effective in one school in which one of us has worked closely as Ofsted testify:

> Opportunities for social development are very good and are a strength of the school. Pupils have very good opportunities to respond to teachers and to other individuals. Language and communication are painstakingly developed. Pupils are enabled to communicate in a variety of ways. *Intensive Interaction* activities improve pupils' attention spans, and encourage them to communicate.
>
> (Ofsted report, Waverley School 17–20 September 2001,
> Ref: 102070, para 48)

Expectations

Links with NC subjects, as well as the intense valuing of pupils, can be demonstrated to teams who are willing to see them. Again, the Ofsted team at Waverley School demonstrates what can be achieved and reported:

> . . . The teaching of language, literacy and communication skills is very good. Children use a variety of ways to communicate, including voice, gestures, simple signs and eye contact. Staff are highly skilled at interpreting, extending and supporting children's attempts to communicate. They have established an environ-

ment, which is sensitive to children's communications, which are acknowledged and listened to with respect.

(Ofsted report, Waverley School 17–20 September 2001, Ref: 102070, para 98)

There is an inconsistency of response though, as Potter and Whittaker (2001: 163) describe from their research on children with autism:

Some Ofsted Inspection teams seem to understand the difficulties [of teaching children with minimal language abilities subjects that are heavily language based] and do not appear to expect the detailed documentation in this area . . . but others expect strict adherence to a subject focus.

Our choices, though, are to expect the worst of the inspection team and become cynical in our efforts to share the practice in which we believe or to prepare for a team that is open and skilled and do all that we can to help them to be open and skilled.

There is room for some optimism that Ofsted are willing to learn from us, particularly when it comes to pupils with PMLD. The 1996/97 Ofsted overview applauded a commitment to the NC and the lack of disapplication from subjects, but commented:

Teachers of pupils with profound and multiple learning difficulties are not clear about how appropriate the full breadth of the National Curriculum is for these pupils. They are unsure in particular about the attention that should be given to foundation subjects such as history and modern foreign languages. Consultations with schools on these matters are taking place at a national level.

(Ofsted, *Standards and Quality in Education 1996/97*, special schools)

We read from this that if convincing positions are offered, then these will be gratefully received.

Monitoring progress

The Ofsted overview report also noted that 'Only half of special schools have satisfactory systems for assessment, recording and reporting.' The QCA's (2001a: 27) framework of encounter; awareness; attention and response; engagement; participation; involvement; and gaining skills and understanding at least offers a structure that is highly compatible with Intensive Interaction. And we know that, in the early years at least, we can use the Early Learning Goals in a meaningful way.

The provision for children aged five years and under is very good. This is because of the high quality teaching and learning, the strong links with families, the quality of learning opportunities provided, and the careful assessment and monitoring of pupils' progress . . . The provision has been strengthened by the clear linking of learning opportunities to the Early Learning Goals and guidance regarding Foundation Stage Curriculum, and a number of new initiatives such as the intensive interaction project and the sensory curriculum.

> (Ofsted report, Waverley School 17–20 September 2001, Ref: 102070, para 90)

Guidance in the QCA (2001a: 25) General Guidelines is also reassuring:

> For pupils with learning difficulties, records of experiences, progress and achievements in relation to targets in their IEPs and curriculum plans should focus on significant responses or ways of learning. A system should be flexible enough to include unexpected or unusual responses, however these occur . . . For pupils with more profound and complex difficulties, comments on the quality of learning are important, to describe, interpret and explain the complexities of individual responses.

Making progress

The last item in our task analysis highlighted the need to demonstrate that progress is indeed happening. We have placed a lot of emphasis on this in the book, with the case studies illustrating both what can be achieved and how it can be shown. Chapter 15 expands on this theme, and we offer practical guidance in this chapter too, but first we offer the reassurance of positive words from Ofsted:

> Pupils' achievements in English are good. They are strongest in speaking and listening, signing and watching . . . The Picture Exchange Communication system (PECS) and Intensive Interaction projects, although relatively new, are beginning to have a very good effect on pupils' progress.

> (Ofsted report, Waverley School 17–20 September 2001, Ref: 102070, para 5)

Policies, planning and recording

School Development Plan

In Chapter 4 we discussed the importance of policy writing as a way of developing and demonstrating clarity of thought about the role of Intensive Interaction in the school and curriculum. We suggested what a school policy on Intensive Interaction might include: the rationale and aims, as well as statements about training, the curriculum, record-keeping and measuring progress. In terms of accountability, a policy helps to explicate the criteria against which we would want to be judged. In this way the policies offer a link between official, imposed evaluation criteria and our own self-imposed criteria.

Central to self-reflective accountability is the School Development Plan. This working document for much of senior management decision-making is vital for setting out our stall. In its forward projections the SDP communicates much about the ethos of a school, what is valued and where the investments of time and money are being made. Ofsted teams spend considerable time scrutinising SDPs, which provide a steering direction for evidence collection. We need to ensure that the strategic vision for the school includes a focus on collaborative working by staff and on key skills, particularly communication, within the curriculum.

The role of schools in securing inclusion is clarified by the QCA National Curriculum Inclusion statement; QCA Curriculum Guidance for pupils with learning difficulties; Ofsted Guidance on Evaluating Inclusion; SEN and Disability Act (2001) and further supporting legislation and guidance. The SDP needs to make explicit the school's interpretation of this in its plans for inclusive practice. As we show in the next chapter, this can also be an opportunity to show how Intensive Interaction and inclusion are related in terms of pedagogy and values.

Policy and long-term planning

The QCA (2001a: 7) state: 'Once agreed, the school aims will inform the development of curriculum plans, provide a focus for the work of the school and establish an essential reference point when reviewing curriculum provision.' It is useful to have a strongly articulated position such as that opening Maskell *et al.*'s (2001: 1) book:

- Every pupil has a fundamental right to be able to communicate.
- Every pupil has the right to develop his or her ability to communicate, at whatever level, and to be given the opportunity to respond to and control his or her environment.

At the next level of detail, after such statements of aim or ethos and the SDP, curriculum policies, teaching and learning policies, or policies for the early years/ primary/secondary department can all specify the school's commitment to Intensive Interaction as an approach. Once specified it will form part of what inspectors and others look for in the school. We can usefully map the expected approach, our preferred approach and school practice to make good practice impossible to miss. The chart in Box 13.1 illustrates the kind of thing we mean.

This kind of documentation places the kinds of skills development flagged up by QCA within a social interaction context. Thus, observation of an Intensive Interaction session would ring lots of bells in terms of coherence with the stated long-term and medium-term plans of the school as well as with QCA guidance.

Medium- and short-term planning: Individual Education Plans

The Individual Education Plans (IEPs), required as part of the *SEN Code of Practice* (DfES 2001), are an ideal place to communicate clearly our intentions and rationale

Teaching and learning policy		
The school's approach to teaching and learning stresses the importance of pupils as active learners. Active learning is supported in all key skills, thinking skills and additional priorities across the curriculum. Pupils are entitled to learning opportunities that are meaningful, stimulating and challenging.		
Opportunities to be actively engaged in **communication** learning will be offered across the curriculum.	Lessons will involve pupils in a range of processes including: • Responding to others • Communicating preferences • Expressing choices • Expressing emotions • Anticipating responses • Sustaining social interactions • Terminating interactions • Initiating interactions	Progress will be monitored through narrative and video records, noting significant developments such as: • new responses • increased range of facial expressions • emerging vocalisations • bodily responses nearing gestures • more effective use of gaze to effect changes in the communicative exchange
Opportunities for actively **working with others** will be offered across the curriculum.	Lessons will involve pupils in a range of processes including: • awareness of others • joint focus • turn-taking • sharing • negotiating rules	Progress will be monitored through narrative and video records, noting significant developments such as: • greater tolerance • spontaneous participation • observing others • waiting for a turn
Opportunities for actively developing **thinking skills** will be offered across the curriculum.	Lessons will involve pupils in a range of processes including: • exploring social agency – what happens if... • exploring variations within familiar interactive games • anticipating – if I vocalise I get a vocal response • remembering – rehearsing familiar games	Progress will be monitored through narrative and video records, noting significant developments such as: • new variations • awareness of cause and effect • looking for an expected response • visually tracking a familiar adult in anticipation of a game

Box 13.1 Teaching and learning policy

for the pupils' involvement with Intensive Interaction. Setting targets may feel a bit uncomfortable with our process approach, but at the IEP level we are not saying what we want to happen in a particular lesson, but where we are heading over a period of time such as a school term. Although we want the flexibility to be child-led in individual interactions, we are likely to have ideas about our interactive aspirations with a pupil, such as developing eye contact, contingent responding, gesture and so on.

Harriet

Target: To develop Harriet's interest in human faces.

Strategy: Daily Intensive Interaction – establishing mutual pleasure while in face-to-face situations, making the most of Harriet's willingness to be close, doing things with our faces that might interest her, seizing opportunities to respond contingently to her facial expressions and signs of interest.

Evidence of progress: would be any of the following – glances at faces during unstructured activities; more sustained looking at faces within interactive sessions; reaching out to faces; mutual gaze.

Progress will be monitored through: narrative records of interactive sessions, including any aspects of facial regard as significant, special notes made of highest and new achievements, analysis of video for quantifiable progress – frequency/incidence/time spent in facial regard.

Box 13.2 Example IEP targets for Harriet

We would advise against being lured into over-tightening objectives into SMART targets (specific, measurable, achievable, relevant). The problem with this degree of tightness is that specificity and measurability tend to work against relevance and meaningfulness. They take away any sense of the pupils' abilities developing in a less controlled, more evolutionary way from the rich social learning environment we provide. Instead, we can assert our own versions of target-setting which retain the essence of interactivity and spontaneity that social/communication learning is all about. Such IEP targets and their measurement might take the form of the examples in Boxes 13.2 and 13.3 for two of the pupils featured in Part Two of this book, Harriet and Jacob.

Lesson planning

The Ofsted handbook (2000) requires inspectors, within an inclusive framework, to include evaluations *in every lesson observed* of how well the teaching meets the needs of all its pupils and students and how well students learn and make progress. A lesson cannot be judged satisfactory if:

- A significant minority of pupils are not engaged in the lesson.
- Basic skills are not well taught.
- Pupils do not know what they are doing.
- Pupils are not making progress.

There is nothing in this that should cause us concern in relation to Intensive Interaction. If we are doing it properly then pupils are likely to be engaged, to be

---

Jacob

Target: To reinforce Jacob's use of his first word (yum).

Strategy: Daily Intensive Interaction sessions in which vocalising will be rehearsed as an important part of Jacob's interactive play; setting up these familiar repertoires as a context in which Jacob can experiment with his sound-making. Operate general interactivity in which all of Jacob's vocalisation and verbalisation is responded to as meaningful communication. Use of yum in 'dialogue' at meal-times.

Evidence of progress: would be any of the following – use of the word in playful interactions; experimentation with the sound of the word; imitation of the word; spontaneous use of the word at meal-times; use of the word with different people.

Progress will be monitored through: narrative records of interactive sessions, including any aspects of verbalisation as significant, diary record for regular noting of when and where verbalisation occurs.

Box 13.3 Example IEP targets for Jacob

learning fundamental skills, to be taking meaning from the experience and to be making progress. Again, we just need to make explicit in our lesson planning the parameters for this. An example is set out in Box 13.4.

Records of the interactions in individual lessons need to be made immediately after the event in order to capture the subtleties and complexities that may constitute evidence of progress and that may inform future interactions. There is no reason why the recording and reflection system advocated in *A Practical Guide to Intensive Interaction* (Nind and Hewett 2001) should not be appropriate in schools (see Box 13.5). There are, of course, endless variations to the basic form shown below which allow teachers to tie this in to their own school's existing systems and to individual and curricular plans.

Parents

We have focused primarily on accountability as part of the inspection framework and as part of our professional responsibilities within the education system. But we are also accountable to our pupils and to their parents or other advocates. The processes of clarifying our policies and planning, and of ensuring we strive for and monitor progress, will also be greatly reassuring for parents. With parents in mind, we need to ensure that what we are doing is transparent for all to see. Parents are quite rightly concerned with their children's attainments in school, but also with

---

Lesson Plan: 13 December 2002 (4 pupils with PMLD)

Aim: To develop the key skill of communication

Specific focus: facial regard

NC/AT links: Personal and social development – interacting and working with others; English NC AT1 level 1 convey simple meanings/listen to others

Venue: carpeted area of classroom

Session time: 20 mins

Resource: the adults themselves

Preparation: area cleared of peripheral equipment; pupils comfortable after toileting and positioned where face-to-face interaction can readily occur; video camera charged and available; discussion of who is causing concern might be a useful target for observation/video.

Warm-up: play familiar short piece of music – aural cue for the session, staff approach pupil with whom they are paired and position themselves well for the individual to see them, up to 5 mins of stillness/quiet if possible to communicate that no other demands are being made.

Main session: Intensive Interaction – individual pairs interact following II principles – taking pauses as led by pupils – using pause to communicate readiness to continue – and if nothing is forthcoming to observe other pairs/video if any interactions are judged significant/interesting. If 2 pairs are paused, adults may swop round to interact with a different pupil.

Cool-down: After most intensive part of the session spend a few moments, sharing space and perhaps gentle physical contact. 2 staff write narrative records while 2 are alert to group and opportunities for follow-up interaction. Swop over.

Evaluation: review if atmosphere was conducive for all, if space and time were sufficient, if staff were sufficiently calm and focused and what progress was made by individual pupils.

Box 13.4 Example lesson plan

their social inclusion and emotional well-being. The best way of showing that these are our priorities too is to involve parents.

Once we get around some of the awkwardness of teachers using nurturing processes usually associated with parenting, we can find that teachers and parents have much to learn from each other about the interactive strategies that are most effective for individuals. Teachers and parents can share stories (and videos) of children's interactive achievements and encourage each other in the reflective and enjoyable processes of Intensive Interaction.

INTERACTION DAILY RECORD

Interaction partners:

Date and time:

Place and situation:

What happened? (describe the sequence)

What was significant? (new, different, possibly progress)

How did it feel? (my response and performance)

Other comments:

Box 13.5 Intensive Interaction recording sheet

CHAPTER 14

Intensive Interaction and Inclusion

The context in which teachers are currently implementing Intensive Interaction in schools is not just one in which accountability is high on people's agendas, it is one in which inclusion has a growing presence, at the level of school rhetoric if not practice. When we are hard at work with our heads down absorbed in our classroom practices and individual pupils, it is tempting to just dismiss inclusion or inclusive education as someone else's issue, to tell ourselves that 'our/my' pupils are too 'special/different/needy'. In this chapter we discuss the ways in which Intensive Interaction is compatible with an ethos of inclusion and how it can be helpful to think about the two together. In this we draw on ideas from a previously published article (Nind and Cochrane 2002). We look at Intensive Interaction in different settings and as a problem-solving and preventative framework. Firstly though, we need to discuss what we mean by inclusion.

Understanding inclusion

In discussing what we mean by inclusion we do not offer a neat consensus definition, instead we need to acknowledge that this is contested ground (Clough 2000); there is no objective truth or certainty about it (Allan 2000). Inclusion and inclusive education are contextual, that is, 'what counts as inclusive in one context may be seen as highly exclusive in another' (Corbett 1999: 53). A pupil with PMLD attending a mainstream school but not enjoying meaningful participation and learning may count as inclusion for those who favour the importance of location, while for others more concerned with process, inclusion may be more about the respect shown for the pupil's difference. Disabled theorists and activists, academics and politicians all make their claim to the terms and use them differently.

In schools it may feel like the drive for inclusion is coming from government as another top-down initiative from those who do not know what it is like at the chalk-face. However, government initiatives may be better understood as responses to the 'the worldwide push for civil rights', and to the now heard voice of disabled people expressing their 'anger about the stigma, degradation and curricular and social limits imposed by the segregated education to which they had been subjected' (Thomas *et al.* 1998: 4). The tide of inclusion has a context that goes beyond Westminster, it is more than a political fashion, and despite some of the backlash expressed by 'responsible inclusionists', it is not a fad that will go away if you keep your head down.

One of the difficulties we face in understanding inclusion is that in some literature (particularly government documents) the terms 'integration' and 'inclusion' are used interchangeably. This can lead us to feel that there is nothing new here and that one afternoon per week spent in a mainstream classroom is sufficient. However, there is some kind of consensus that 'the change from integration to inclusion is much more than a fashionable change in politically correct semantics' (Mittler 2000a: 10). While integration was/is about preparing pupils for placement in ordinary schools with the pupil, not the school, having to do the adapting, inclusion is more generally understood as schools readying themselves for more diverse pupils, even radically reforming their systems. The schools and pupil have to fit with each other, rather than the pupil having to fit with an unchanged curriculum and organisation (Barton 1995). When we begin to understand inclusion as 'a commitment to removing all barriers to the full participation of each child as a valued, unique individual' (Alliance for Inclusive Education 2002), then we begin to see how pupils with SLD/PMLD and Intensive Interaction might feature.

Inclusion, then, encapsulates genuine participation and stresses equality as well as location. Once there is an onus on schools to fit with pupils, there is a realisation that pupils' differences do not have to be minimised, but that their difference is treated as welcome and ordinary. This shifts attention to processes, which is, of course, highly compatible with our focus on process in interactive approaches. Both Intensive Interaction and inclusion are concerned with what goes on between teachers and pupils (and between different pupils). Both are concerned with increasing the processes that allow connections to be made and decreasing the pressures for exclusion.

The concept of inclusion as an active process fits also with the common view of inclusion as a journey – something that people work towards and continually strive for. Ballard (1995) has argued that there is no such thing as an inclusive school, just a limitless process of inclusion. Similarly Ainscow (2000: 41) explains:

> I have a transformative approach to inclusion which involves asking how we can actually transform the education system, such that it is more capable of developing its capacity to reach out to all learners in a way which suggests it is an ever-ongoing process that never ends in that sense.

Transforming the curriculum and the pedagogical style in order to reach out to all learners very accurately describes what went on at Harperbury School in the early days of developing Intensive Interaction. It very probably describes what teachers working to implement Intensive Interaction in the current context are doing also. Working with (or being) pupils who are pre-verbal can place us at the margins of educational life, whether this be in a special school, a resource base or even in a mainstream school. Issues of placement can be beyond our control as teachers, but issues of process are not. We discuss here how using Intensive Interaction can help to increase the inclusive capacity of teachers in whatever context they work.

Intensive Interaction as a collaborative problem-solving framework

For us, the connections between Intensive Interaction and inclusion were not made explicit until, in 1999, Steve Cochrane approached Melanie Nind about working together on an action research project in his local education authority focused on Intensive Interaction and inclusion. For this LEA adviser the connection was obvious:

- Intensive Interaction could help to keep pupils presenting extreme challenges in local contexts rather than be moved out of borough to residential provision.
- This would retain resources within the LEA to support further inclusion.
- An important part of the process of inclusion is addressing what goes on between pupils 'who fall outside the routine competence and confidence of teachers' and those teachers, whether they be teachers in special or mainstream schools. Intensive Interaction provides a practical means of enhancing teachers' competence and confidence.

(Nind and Cochrane 2002)

From here, once we move beyond a naïve placement model of inclusion, the compatibility of Intensive Interaction and inclusion are self-evident. Intensive Interaction is a positive response to pupil diversity. It focuses on making the curriculum fit the pupil and not the pupil fit the curriculum. And it supports teachers and empowers them to make their own connections with the pupil, rather than undermines them with notions of an expert other who will come in and offer some specialist intervention.

Porter's distinctions between traditional and inclusionary practice (adapted by Thomas *et al.* 1998) can help us to think this through:

Traditional (may include integration)	**Inclusionary**
• Focus on student	• Focus on classroom
• Assessment of student by specialist	• Examine teaching/learning factors
• Diagnostic/prescriptive outcomes	• Collaborative problem-solving
• Student programme	• Strategies for teachers
• Placement in appropriate programme	• Adaptive and supportive regular classroom environment
• Needs of 'special' students	• Rights of all students
• Changing/remedying the subject	• Changing the school
• Benefits to the student with SEN of being integrated	• Benefits to all students of including all
• Professionals, specialist expertise and formal support	• Informal support and the expertise of mainstream teachers
• Technical interventions (special teaching, therapy)	• Good teaching for all

Intensive Interaction was designed in a special, segregated context for pupils with a special set of needs and circumstances and because of this we might think of it as a technical intervention or special teaching, thus belonging to a traditional approach. However, Intensive Interaction is also 'firmly enmeshed with principles of good teaching for all' as it is based on the intuitive pedagogy that is 'good teaching for all at the early developmental levels' (Nind and Cochrane 2002: 188). From this perspective it belongs within the inclusionary paradigm. Moreover, Intensive Interaction's claim to belonging on this side of the divide is strengthened by the essence of the approach as about examining teaching and learning factors, using a collaborative problem-solving approach and developing strategies for teachers. The onus is less on remediating the pupil and more on enhancing the skills of the interactive partners and teaching staff.

Just as Ainscow (2000: 39) reflects on his own transformation as he 'moved from being concerned with particular children to being concerned with contexts', when we use Intensive Interaction we take responsibility for the social environment of our pupils. We shift our focus on to what is and is not working in our interactions and pedagogy, which is also highly compatible with much of the emphasis on school improvement. In common with all other interactive approaches, however, it is less concerned with outcomes than with active learners and learning processes. Intensive Interaction provides an interactive lens through which to view the challenge of particular pupils and of the curriculum. Importantly, for inclusion, it locates the problem and solution in the school/curriculum rather than in the pupil.

We can illustrate this focus with examples from the action research project and another that followed on from it. Schools unused to Intensive Interaction and similar approaches were more likely to see the pupils beyond their routine confidence and competence through a 'normative' lens (Ainscow 1999: 6) – as intruders for whom some add-on curriculum adaptation was needed (Nind and Cochrane 2002). For the school staff already using Intensive Interaction, however, the obvious response to gaps in their confidence and competence was to observe each other interacting, link up experienced and less experienced practitioners to share ideas, and to see such collaborative partnership work as their key resource. When a mainstream early years department sought help from the authority because they had a number of pupils with limited communication and language abilities, a *transactional* rather than *deficit* model was adopted. Thus, the bi-directional influences in communication difficulties and communication learning were fully recognised. This was a communication issue for pupils *and* staff and our focus was to be on the communication environment and the verbal and interactive behaviour of the adults rather than on individual problems. We used the concepts of optimal interactive styles from studies of caregiver–infant interaction that we use in Intensive Interaction to inform our observation, discussion, action and reflection. This led to efforts to make verbal interactions less adult-dominated and more child-led, less directive and more responsive. Thus, in our inclusive, collaborative problem-solving approach we set about making the learning environment more effective, without pathologising or segregating individual children.

Intensive Interaction in inclusive settings

The examples we have given come from both special school and mainstream education settings. In these illustrations Intensive Interaction helped the schools to cope with their diverse and changing pupil populations in a positive way. It helped staff to feel good about their efficacy and, therefore, to feel good about the pupils. Such feelings of efficacy contribute to positive long-term learning relationships and to keeping the pupils in their local environments. The projects were small scale and not part of any radical reconstruction of the education system. In this LEA schools for pupils with SLD/PMLD were not being closed down, but they were being developed as resources for mainstream schools who were taking pupils with SLD from their local areas. In other LEAs we are far more likely to find pupils for whom Intensive Interaction is appropriate within the mainstream. And some readers will be asking: can the two come together?

The challenge that Intensive Interaction poses for teachers in mainstream contexts depends fundamentally on the school's ethos. A recent approach for help with Intensive Interaction came from a mainstream nursery school that had pupils with autism and that felt that Intensive Interaction would be far more in keeping with their nursery education traditions than other more formalised approaches. In the early years there need be no problems. This kind of compatibility would not lead secondary schools to seek Intensive Interaction, however. Indeed, as we have argued, child-centred curricula and subject-centred curricula are the antithesis of each other. Problems arise beyond the early years from a normative framework in which we have narrow age-related expectations, and the solution lies in changing this mindset.

When we developed Intensive Interaction, changed practice followed a changed mindset. We stopped thinking about 'How can we stop her doing X and teach her to do Y as a subskill of Z?' We started thinking, instead, 'If we could make ourselves interesting and accessible, then we could begin to play actively together and form a relationship, and together we could move into new areas of social and communicative competence.' Changing the mindset is again essential to inclusive education. We have to stop thinking about how we can fit these children with these deficits into our systems with the minimum disturbance to them and to other pupils. And we need to start thinking about how can we radically reorganise and rethink what we do so that all these diverse pupils can learn effectively together and from each other. In this latter scenario pupils needing Intensive Interaction challenge us to think about how we can make learning active and meaningful for all pupils.

Inclusive schools will not be places in which, for example, all 13-year-olds are sitting together doing the same thing at the same time. Much more imagination and creativity are needed. In bringing something new to our pedagogy we must not be afraid of deconstructing that which is already there. Thomas and Loxley (2001) have contended that to construct inclusion we need to deconstruct special education. Culham and Nind (in press) have argued that normalisation is not a safe platform on which to build inclusion. At Harperbury School, Intensive Interaction was not added on to the behavioural approaches already in existence; it replaced them. Teachers implementing Intensive Interaction need to take risks. This can be scary, but it is also enormously liberating and energising.

Adult services for people with learning difficulties are grappling with the drive to support people to live ordinary lives and all that this means. Many providers are recognising that valuing ordinary experiences and community participation does not mean conformity and sacrificing experiences needed for quality of life and continued development for the sake of appearances. Inclusive schools grapple with similar tensions and old ideas about schooling are incredibly resilient. The starting point for a pupil attending an inclusive school and participating in Intensive Interaction is a school ethos that says:

'Yes, please come and we as adults, pupils and our institution as a whole will adapt as best we can in order to meet your needs.' This may mean adapting our attitudes and thinking, the curriculum, classroom organisation, furniture and equipment and/or the building . . .

(Phillips *et al.* in press)

We can put a child in a mainstream context but that does not mean he/she is included in the sense of being part of the school community. Community is the ties and connections we have with others that give us a sense of belonging, which in turn helps with our emotional well-being (Cole and Lloyd 2002). Intensive Interaction can help when such connections do not come easily.

Best deals

Corbett (1997: 56) has questioned the usefulness of the inclusion–exclusion dichotomy because it 'fails to reflect the various stages of in-between-ness' that exist in real contexts. She reminds us of the untidy compromises that parents and teachers seek as the best deal in difficult circumstances. An example of the best deal might be a child going to the nearest accessible ordinary school, even if this is not the nearest school per se. In terms of Intensive Interaction and inclusion, the best deal for the moment might be working with an inclusive mindset in a segregated environment, or using interactive processes to enhance the education of pupils while acknowledging that a more diverse pupil group would further enrich the classroom interactions and reflective pedagogy. Interestingly, the Intensive Interaction web site has recently included a discussion of mainstream pupils as Intensive Interaction partners:

> It has been a very moving experience to witness Intensive Interaction between Year 6 pupils from a mainstream school and our pupils who have severe/complex learning difficulties. What was great was how naturally they took to it and made comments like 'he really looked into my eyes – it made me tingle' and 'I like making that noise as well.'
>
> (www.IntensiveInteraction.co.uk)

For teachers in special environments working with apparently special approaches, it is important for us to remember that we are involved with inclusion and to feel part of it. Teachers who are working to bring the curriculum alive for pupils who challenge them are taking part in a process of inclusion, even if they are living with the contradiction of also being part of a process of segregation. It is useful for us to remember that inclusion is not a 'once-and-for-all event' (Allan 2000: 31). It is continually being negotiated. We are unlikely to find a school that has reached the end of its journey to being inclusive, but we will find 'moments of inclusion' and probably more of exclusion (Benjamin *et al.* 2002). It can be helpful to think of every interaction we have with a pupil as having the potential to be a moment of inclusion or exclusion. We can use our interactive and reflective abilities to make activities meaningful, to create moments of connection from incidental interactions, to create anticipation and involvement and to facilitate spontaneous communication and participation. As individuals we can make a difference. But change has to be systemic as well as individual

(Thomas *et al.* 1998) and the teamwork and collaborative reflection involved in Intensive Interaction are great for bringing about more whole-scale changes.

Intensive Interaction as preventative/inclusive pedagogy

Booth (1992: 39) has stressed that difficulties in learning arise when there is a mismatch between the learner and the teaching/task/materials: 'They indicate a breakdown in the relationship between pupils and curricula.' When we pitch our interactions wrongly we make learning difficult for our pupils; we begin a process of exclusion. Conversely, when we achieve a good 'interactive fit' we enable them to participate and to engage in learning to learn. In this way we can think of Intensive Interaction as a preventative measure.

The case studies in this book (and reported in more detail in Kellett 2000; Kellett 2001; Kellett 2003) are the first to show the impact of Intensive Interaction on children in the early and primary years. We can see the alternative educational pathways that pupils like Sam and Jacob might take: a journey towards further isolation and self-injury on the one hand, or being drawn into learning partnerships on the other. A key deciding factor for which route the pupil takes is whether or not we achieve access to communication; whether or not we establish an interactive style that is nurturing and puts the teacher–learner pair on to a 'virtuous' circle (Ware 1996).

We can prevent processes of exclusion from becoming established with good pedagogy. Slee (1999: 200) has talked about the 'pedagogy of recognition', where the curriculum is one in which diverse learners can recognise their own experiences and identities. His concern that inclusive education must engage with and represent pupils' identities so that they can recognise themselves in the curriculum has relevance for us. The curriculum can marginalise pupils with SLD just as it can marginalise travellers and pupils from minority ethnic heritage. Although much more simple than envisaged by Slee, one of the ways in which Intensive Interaction offers a pedagogy of recognition is by starting with and celebrating what the pupil does and who he/she is. When we use pupils' sounds and movements and rhythms in our interactive play we are offering a point of connection across what might otherwise be a huge divide. We are showing respect for the pupils' difference and a willingness to engage with that difference.

Some inclusionists have likened inclusion to democracy. Lipsky and Gartner (1999: 21) go as far as to say that 'inclusive education is not merely a characteristic of a democratic society, it is essential to it'. The point here is that all pupils should enjoy active participation in a school community as this is a matter of being a full member of society and a question of citizenship. This makes a farce of the argument that we should exclude young children from their local communities so that we can more efficiently teach them skills to participate in their communities as adults. We learn best in context; we learn about participation by participating. The active and interactive learning we are concerned with is about empowerment, democracy and citizenship as this learning inevitably involves the teacher and learner in sharing and negotiating power (Collins *et al.* 2002). When we 'do' Intensive Interaction, we are 'doing' citizenship.

Intensive Interaction shares with other good pedagogy a coalition between what the teacher and learner bring to the learning situation. Corbett (2001) has described inclusive pedagogy as 'connective pedagogy' – a way of working that connects with individual learners and their way of learning, that in turn connects them with the curriculum and wider community. Connective pedagogy 'opens up creative possibilities to learn' (Corbett 2001: 56) by recognising the importance of affective learning. Intensive Interaction fosters emotional engagement with learning and between teacher and learner. This may be uncomfortable for some, but we know from listening to disaffected pupils (Kinder *et al.* 1996) and to pupils who have been resilient and succeeded against the odds (Jackson and Martin 1998) that an emotional connection is vital to staying connected to education. Building this strongly in the early interactions is part of the preventive power of the approach.

Index for Inclusion

The Index for Inclusion (Booth *et al.* 2000) is a government-endorsed set of materials to support schools in a process of self-review to become more inclusive. It covers the dimensions of school cultures, policies and practices. While the indicators of inclusion and associated questions provide useful prompts for thinking and action, however, the pupils for whom Intensive Interaction is most appropriate are noticeable by their absence. For example:

C1.1 Lessons are responsive to student diversity –
x) Is there a variety of activities, including discussion, oral presentation, writing, drawing, problem-solving, use of library, audio visual materials, practical task and information technology?

C1.2 Lessons are made accessible to students –
iii) Is technical vocabulary explained and practised during lessons?

C1.5 Students learn collaboratively –
vi) Do students learn how to compile a joint report from the different contributions of a group?

We can find indicators that would include a greater diversity of pupil ability, including PMLD. And there are questions that link neatly with the whole school audit in Chapter 11, such as:

C.2.3 Staff expertise is fully utilised –
iv) Do teachers with particular skills and knowledge offer their help to others?

Dimension: Evolving Inclusive Practices

C.1 Orchestrating learning

Indicator: Lessons are responsive to student diversity
- Is it acknowledged that for some students the lesson is the interactions they take part in?
- Do lessons recognise the significance of process for individuals as well as product?

Indicator: Lessons are made accessible to all students
- Do lessons enable each student to start from what they know and can do?
- Do lessons allow students to rehearse interactions within their safe repertoire?

Indicator: Lessons develop an understanding of difference
- Do staff and other students recognise that some students need interactions that apparently break the rules of age-appropriateness?
- Are idiosyncratic means of communication valued?

Indicator: Students are actively involved in their own learning
- Is non-verbal feedback from students recognised and responded to?
- Are students enabled to make meaningful choices about the nature of their interactive episodes?
- Are students encouraged to spontaneously initiate interactions and to end them when they are ready?

C.2 Mobilising resources

Indicator: School resources are distributed fairly to support inclusion
- Are staff and their interactive abilities recognised as key resources?
- Are these resources looked after and valued?
- Is time made available for quality one-to-one interaction as needed?

Indicator: Community resources are known and drawn upon
- Are the interactive abilities of family members and friends recognised and used?
- Are ideas for interactive games shared?
- Do staff make use of opportunities to learn about cultural differences in interactions?

Indicator: Student difference is used as a resource for teaching and learning
- Are students encouraged to interact with each other in different ways?
- Are spontaneous and intuitive attempts by students to interact with others valued and developed?

Box 14.1 Ideas for further questions in an adapted Index for Inclusion

vi) Are there formal as well as informal opportunities for staff to resolve concerns over students by drawing on each other's experience?

But a useful exercise for schools might be to draw up 'further questions' for use as indicators of inclusion that reflect inclusion of pupils with PMLD more centrally, and the school staff's own concepts of inclusive pedagogy. Box 14.1 shows the outcomes of some of our own thinking on this.

Being idealist

For some teachers their sense of pragmatism will make this chapter difficult. In some ways it is more a chapter about words and ideas than about practical advice. We do not apologise for this, as we need to do things in our heads before we can do things in our classrooms. For readers who find the idea of pupils with PMLD doing Intensive Interaction in inclusive settings too idealistic it is worth remembering Mittler's (2000b: 105) reflection:

> If someone had said to me, when I was training as a clinical psychologist, the day will come before you retire when people with Down syndrome will get GCSEs, or the day will come when you will be invited by people with Down syndrome to their meeting which they will chair and run, I would have thought they were being 'unrealistic'.

Both of these things have happened, and more. Some of the kinds of inclusion we have been discussing are already happening and those that are not are just a leap of the imagination away.

PART FOUR

Research Frontier

CHAPTER 15

Intensive Interaction and Research: Why Is It Important?

Introduction

The rationale for including this section in the book is twofold. Firstly we want to encourage more practitioners in the field to undertake research. Our aims are:

- to make the research process more accessible to practitioners
- to value the research contributions of practitioners
- to raise the profile of practitioner research.

Secondly we want to draw attention to the need for more evaluative research on Intensive Interaction. The children we work with do not form a homogenous group. The severity and complexity of their learning difficulties makes it improbable that representative or 'typical' sample matches can be found and renders them unsuitable for many large-scale research enterprises. Hence much of the evaluative research that has already been undertaken relies on individual case study and it takes many of these to build up an overall picture of efficacy. Six are published in this volume and the earlier major evaluation comprised a further six (Nind 1993; 1996). While not formalised as research projects, further case studies appear in *Access to Communication* (Nind and Hewett 1994) and *Interaction in Action* (Hewett and Nind 1998). Other published efficacy case studies are listed in Chapter 2, but there is a great need for many more. Furthermore, if Intensive Interaction is to be associated with optimum outcomes for maximum numbers, it must be applicable to changing educational and political climates and continue to move forward and evolve. Thus, in addition to efficacy studies, research also needs to address how Intensive Interaction is being used and implemented. These kinds of investigation lend themselves readily to action research.

There are three chapters in this section. This first chapter explores the rationale for research, why it is important and how it links to Intensive Interaction. The second chapter is a step-by-step guide to help those embarking on their own evaluation study.

The third is a short chapter that identifies some issues of practice, coordination and management which might form the basis of action research projects. There are many professional development courses that require reflective or evaluative assignment components. Teachers studying for Masters degrees or those involved in Best Practice Research Projects [www.teachernet.gov.uk/Professional_Development/opportunities/bprs] may like to consider Intensive Interaction as a research topic.

What is research?

One of us recently asked a group of nine-year-olds what they thought research was. Although their responses were quite diverse, each pupil, without exception, included two common words somewhere in their definition: 'finding out'. And in essence 'finding out' is precisely what research is all about. Research is about asking questions, exploring issues and reflecting on findings. It is concerned with extending our knowledge and pursuing 'truth'. There is a moral imperative for research to be purposive and an expectation that new knowledge generated will be used for greater social good: 'What is important to those who carry out research – whatever its scale – is that it should somehow *make a difference*' (Clough and Nutbrown 2002: 6, their emphasis).

Research creates knowledge by exploring issues and finding answers to questions that might not otherwise have been asked. Some problems seem straightforward but their exploration can turn such expectations on their head and give rise to new, unforeseen questions that result in new lines of research. An example of this is the way in which research into the history of learning disability has led to questions about who owns the history and who knows; the experiences of professionals and of people with learning difficulties are quite different (Jackson 2000). The word 'research' is sometimes off-putting for practitioners who have an impression that it is something done by academic 'experts'. This need not be the case and we hope to demystify some of the esoteric baggage sometimes associated with research and promote the important contributions that can be made to the body of 'real world' research by practitioners in the field. As Robson (2002) argues the word 'research' is simply another word for 'enquiry'.

> I have tried to walk the tightrope between stressing how easy the enquiry task is – because much of what you have to do is common sense – and how difficult it is for exactly the same reason. The core skills are watching people and talking to them. These are based on very common human activities and any reader will have had extensive experience of them. The trick is to avoid 'deskilling' yourself by devaluing this experience, while appreciating the need to do these things with an uncommon degree of both system and sensitivity.
>
> (p. xv)

Research and truth

We all experience the world in different ways. We have different perspectives and we disagree about what is true in our different experiences. So how can we establish the truth between different and often conflicting experiences? Research *systematically* and *sceptically* investigates claims to truth whereby even commonplace assumptions are treated with doubt.

Research activity also has to be *ethical*, to have regard for the interests and needs of participants and those upon whom the findings of the research might have an impact. In doing research we have to be frank and critical about what, how and why our research is taking place. We have a duty to make our observations accurately and clearly, whether or not such observations accord with our previous assumptions. We have to describe the circumstances in which an observation or measurement is made and who makes the observation and expect our methods and findings to be open to scrutiny. This concern to be systematic, sceptical and ethical is what distinguishes research from other types of investigation undertaken by, for example, journalists and barristers who very much use their investigative findings to advocate and represent a particular view. They deliberately create evidence and argument to support the view rather than to doubt or challenge that view. This does not mean their view is necessarily false but it could mean that they fail to acknowledge when it might be. It is these reasons that equate good research with a 'better sort of truth'. None of this is straightforward, however, as increasingly disabled and feminist researchers (among others) are making explicit the values position that informs their research, which is often conducted to benefit specific groups.

Different types of research

Research is frequently divided into 'positivist' and 'interpretive' paradigms. Positivism is concerned with objectivity and controllability, with the ability to predict and to measure and to ascribe causality. It is sometimes referred to as the scientific model or associated with the natural sciences; it is also associated more with quantitative methods. There have been some strong reactions against this kind of research, particularly in educational contexts. One area of criticism concerns the extent to which findings can be valid because of the diversity of interpretation involved and the social situations in which interpersonal interactions take place. Other critics have questioned the logic of some positivist research that assumes human social life consists of fixed, mechanical causal relationships. Such criticisms have stimulated more open-ended research within what is known as the 'interpretive' paradigm.

Interpretive research focuses on understanding and interpreting the world in terms of its actors (Cohen *et al.* 2000) and has a strong emphasis on exploring the nature of particular phenomena rather than testing hypotheses about them. It is associated more with qualitative methods, and is sometimes characterised by unstructured data, small numbers of cases and descriptive analysis. Those who adopt an interpretive stance question positivist assumptions and vice versa. It can, therefore, be most useful to think about research approaches in terms of fitness for purpose: Is this a valid way to approach this question? Or even: Is this a valid question?

Criticisms of both positivist and interpretive paradigms have led to the emergence of several different, alternative paradigms. Paradigm issues are being debated and are in a state of development and change. One alternative paradigm is what has become known as 'critical enquiry research'. This approach is emancipatory and is concerned with the political and ideological contexts in which research enquiry is undertaken: the just rights of participants and real world relevance:

> Its intention [critical theory] is not merely to give an account of society and behaviour but to realize a society that is based on equality and democracy for all its members. Its purpose is not merely to understand situations and phenomena but to change them. In particular it seeks to emancipate the disempowered, to redress inequality and to promote individual freedoms within a democratic society.
>
> (Cohen *et al.* 2000: 28)

Within the education context this model has become known as 'critical educational research'. It exposes educational inequalities and the ways in which the educational system reinforces wider social inequalities. According to Cohen *et al.* (2000), it examines and interrogates issues such as:

> the relationships between school and society – how schools perpetuate or reduce inequality; the social construction of knowledge and curricula, who defines worthwhile knowledge, what ideological interests this serves, and how this reproduces inequality in society; how power is produced and reproduced through education; whose interests are served by education and how legitimate these are.
>
> (p. 28)

All three paradigms are appropriate to Intensive Interaction research studies and can be used to ask different kinds of questions. The positivist style is reflected in, for example, the rigorous, quasi-experimental design of efficacy evaluations undertaken by Nind (1996) and Kellett (2001). These have provided important bodies of evidence that functionally link Intensive Interaction to the promotion of sociability and communication. The interpretive style is reflected in, for example, Hewett and Nind's (1998) *Interaction in Action*, an edited volume of practitioner and parent accounts of their experiences of Intensive Interaction. The critical enquiry style is reflected in, for example, a recent symposium in the *European Journal of Special*

Needs Education where issues concerning inclusion, Intensive Interaction and OSI/stereotyped behaviours were debated by Nind and Kellett, Goldbart, Harris and Hogg (2002).

Why is research important?

With so few teaching staff and so much active work to be done at grass roots level, it is not unreasonable to question whether we should be undertaking research at all. Could the time, effort and money it consumes be better spent on more resources in the classroom? Why is research so important? Research has three crucial dimensions:

- Its innovative and exploratory character can bring about beneficial change.
- Its sceptical enquiry can result in poor or unethical practice being questioned.
- Its rigorous and systematic nature extends knowledge and promotes problem-solving.

Research is also beneficial for our own self-development both as human beings and as professionals. Asking questions like 'How can I improve my own practice?' engages us in a perpetual cycle of professional development that goes hand in hand with research. Moreover, it can result in some theory or abstract ideas being generated through practice rather than the other way round.

Research ethics

'Ethics' are sometimes confused with 'morals' and a distinction needs to be drawn. Both concern right and wrong: 'morals' relate to whether or not certain actions are consistent with accepted notions of right and wrong, 'ethics' refer to general principles about what *should* be done (Robson 2002). Ethical issues are present at the very beginning of undertaking research and permeate the entire research process. There are ethics involved in early decisions, such as the kind of questions that are formulated and the individuals who are included or, just as significantly, excluded. There are obvious ethical issues in gaining informed consent (and again, significantly, in issues of informed 'dissent'), in how we deal with confidentiality and how we responsibly handle the knowledge we acquire. Ethics committees are now commonplace in many settings and you may find that you have to get formal ethics clearance before embarking on a research project. If this is not the case then it is wise to talk about research plans with colleagues and senior managers or a research supervisor. Robson (2002: 69) usefully summarises ten ethically questionable practices to be cognisant of:

1. Involving people without their knowledge or consent
2. Coercing them to participate

3. Withholding information about the true nature of the research
4. Otherwise deceiving the participant
5. Inducing participants to commit acts diminishing their self-esteem
6. Violating rights of self-determination (e.g. in studies seeking to promote individual change)
7. Exposing participants to physical or mental stress
8. Invading privacy
9. Withholding benefits from some participants (e.g. in comparison groups)
10. Not treating participants fairly, with consideration or with respect.

Ethics are particularly important for the work we are engaged in because we are working with children who have severe learning difficulties and, as such, are highly vulnerable individuals. It is advisable to inform all participants (and guardians of participants) of this exception to confidentiality clauses at the outset. There may be fine judgements to make about how ethical or otherwise some activities you uncover are, e.g. whether abuse of power or professional neglect constitutes a risk to individuals.

The next chapter gives guidance on undertaking an efficacy evaluation study. Many of the issues raised here, including ethical concerns, will be addressed in this context. Efficacy is only one type of evaluation study and there are many more that are applicable to Intensive Interaction. Reading Chapter 16 may give you some ideas but a few examples are included below:

- What works in Intensive Interaction?
- Does my practice lead to these desired outcomes?
- Does my practice lead to other outcomes?
- How does my new practice compare with my old?
- How do my team find using Intensive Interaction?
- What do parents think of Intensive Interaction?
- What aspects of Intensive Interaction practice impact on its effectiveness?

CHAPTER 16

Undertaking an Intensive Interaction Efficacy Evaluation Study: Step-by-Step Guidance

Introduction

In this chapter we set out step-by-step guidance for anyone wishing to undertake an efficacy evaluation study similar to the ones featured in this book. Our intention in doing this is not to be prescriptive or patronising but to make the research process more transparent and less daunting to novice researchers. Experienced researchers may find this chapter less useful and prefer to move on to Chapter 17 where we explore some ideas for action research projects.

Here we look at one aspect of evaluation in detail – we evaluate whether Intensive Interaction achieves its desired outcomes in developing progress in social and communication development. This research study requires:

- a valid and reliable means of measuring small amounts of progress
- a valid and reliable means of comparing such measurements before and during Intensive Interaction.

Gaining informed consent

An obvious starting point is choosing a pupil whom you think would benefit from Intensive Interaction and deciding who is going to be her/his interactive partner for the purposes of measuring progress. We are assuming that this person has been trained in the principles and practices of Intensive Interaction and that in practice this person is working as part of a team. Before going any further the informed consent of parents or guardians *and the pupil her/himself* would need to be gained. Ethical issues with regard to gaining this consent have occupied us in lengthy reflection (see Kellett and Nind 2001). It is important to make the participant/parents fully aware of the aims, rationale and content of any proposed research project so that they can make an informed judgement about the giving of consent. An example of a written information summary for parents appears in Box 16.1. It includes a

---

Intensive Interaction Research Project – Information for Parents

What is Intensive Interaction?
Intensive Interaction is a teaching approach developed by Melanie Nind and Dave Hewett which has been shown to be particularly effective in promoting communication and sociability in individuals with severe and complex learning difficulties. It is a gentle and respectful approach based on the process of caregiver–infant interaction and acknowledges the need to develop the very beginnings of sociability and communication. Intensive Interaction has been widely documented and evaluated (please see attached reading list) and evidence is growing regarding the beneficial outcomes. (There is no evidence to suggest non-beneficial outcomes.) There is a continuing need to evaluate its effectiveness and to understand it further.

What will the project involve for my child?
We have incorporated Intensive Interaction into the teaching philosophy and practice of our school and [insert name of member of staff who is to work with pupil X] has been trained in the principles and practice of the approach. [If you are doing this as an assignment for a professional development course, state this here and indicate whether or not a supervisor is involved.] With your permission I would like to video [pupil X] on a regular basis over a period of [X] terms so that we can analyse her/his progress. The video recording will take place in the normal classroom environment within a routine class lesson. The video tapes are entirely confidential and will only be seen by members of staff who are working with [X] [indicate if a research supervisor will also see material] and will be available to yourself[ves] should you wish to see any of the material.

Will we be informed of the outcome of the project?
Yes, you will be given summary feedback at the end of the project and I will be happy to answer queries at any time during the project.

Consent
You may find some of the literature in the attached reading list helpful. If you are happy for [pupil X] to be involved in the study please could you sign the attached consent form.

Suggested Reading

Hewett, D. & Nind, M. (eds) (1998) *Interaction in Action: Reflections on the Use of Intensive Interaction.* London: David Fulton.

Kellett, M. & Nind, M. (2003) *Implementing Intensive Interaction in Schools: Guidance for Practitioners, Managers and Coordinators.* London: David Fulton.

Nind, M. & Hewett, D. (2001) *A Practical Guide to Intensive Interaction.* Kidderminster: BILD publications.

Nind, M. & Hewett, D. (1994) *Access to Communication: Developing the Basics of Communication in People with Severe Learning Difficulties Through Intensive Interaction.* London: David Fulton.

Nind, M. (1996) 'Efficacy of Intensive Interaction: Developing sociability and communication in people with severe and complex learning difficulties using an approach based on caregiver–infant interaction'. *European Journal of Special Educational Needs,* **11**(1), 48–66.

Box 16.1 Information sheet for parents and guardians

description of Intensive Interaction accompanied by a list of recommended reading. It is also important to make clear to parents that they can withdraw their child from the research study at any time, for any reason.

However, giving parents full and honest information and ensuring there is no coercion does not fully discharge our ethical responsibility. There is a further duty to ensure that the pupil her/himself is comfortable with participation. A useful additional step is to involve a 'circle of trusted people' such as siblings, peer group friends and a wide range of support staff, who understand the pupil, care about her/him and recognise when he/she might be unhappy or uncomfortable. Facilitating open communication along these lines ensures the ongoing and 'informed' consenting status of participants whose learning difficulties are severe and complex (Gillman *et al.* 1997).

Establishing a baseline phase

In order to make a judgement about efficacy we need to be able to compare two conditions: one that uses Intensive Interaction and one that does not. An element of research that is crucially important is what we call **validity**. We have to make sure that we are actually measuring what we set out to measure and that any comparisons we make with other conditions are fair and valid otherwise our findings will be unsound. For example, we cannot draw comparisons about the efficacy of Intensive Interaction by comparing participation in an Intensive Interaction session with participation in a school assembly. There are too many differences (or, in research terms, too many variables) – one is more passive than the other, one involves greater numbers than the other, each is in a different location etc. With so many variables it is not possible to isolate Intensive Interaction as the factor linked to any potential progress. To be able to do this we have to control the number of variables. A valid comparison would be between two one-to-one interactive sessions of similar length in similar locations where the only real difference in the conditions is that one of them consciously uses the principles and practices of Intensive Interaction.

Our experience from doing evaluative studies in schools suggests that an ideal baseline phase length is six weeks with three or four weeks as a minimum. Less than this would mean that before and after comparisons may be using atypical performances, such as an 'off day'. With three or more measures we can begin to get a feel for what is normal and for any trends that are happening. We can make predictions about the kinds of development we might expect over the next four weeks without Intensive Interaction and compare this with what happens when the approach is used. The purpose of the baseline phase then is to gather data that can then be compared with data gathered in the Intensive Interaction sessions (we call this the 'intervention phase'). If you run your evaluative project for two terms then you might be looking at an intervention phase of about 20 weeks.

Choosing your measuring tools

To answer the evaluation question posed regarding whether social and communication development is enhanced we need a means of measuring sociability and communication. Our advice, particularly if you are carrying out a small-scale evaluative study and have little support, is to keep this simple and manageable. While we may surmise that more complex developments are taking place in the pupil's understanding of the world, our desire for research evidence may mean we need to focus on that which we can readily observe and even quantify. The number and kinds of socially interactive behaviours you choose to observe will vary according to how much time you can devote to this study. We suggest that three or four is a working minimum. Some good examples from previous evaluation studies are:

- looking at/towards the face;
- eye contact;
- attending to a joint focus;
- making/continuing/reciprocating social contact through touch;
- contingent vocalisation (vocalising in response to an initiative by the interactive partner);
- initiating social contact with another individual;
- contingent happy expression (in response to an initiative by the interactive partner);
- engagement (a state of absorbed emotional or intellectual arousal and 'connection' with another person).

Gathering your data

While measurement of progress can be done by observing in real time, there are great advantages to gathering data on video for analysis later. Gathering video data will involve setting up a video camera where the Intensive Interaction is to take place. The camera needs to capture images of all potentially interactive behaviour and although the face is crucially important do not neglect other expressive parts of the body such as hands and feet. Ideally, the filming is best done by a colleague. You will need to decide how often you are going to film – we recommend weekly if possible, or fortnightly if this is more feasible. More frequently than this will make the analysis process too onerous for a small-scale project and less frequently than fortnightly will generate insufficient data from which to draw conclusions. In a 15-minute session that includes a warm-up and a cool-down we suggest you record the middle five minutes. It takes a long time to analyse each minute of video film so do not be tempted to be too ambitious, either with the length of session you record or the number of social behaviours you choose to observe.

Coding the data

Analysing the video and coding the data is the onerous and time-consuming part of the evaluation. The social behaviours of pupils who feature in this book were ana-lysed on a per second basis in more than one behavioural situation so the individ-ual coding judgements ran into thousands each week. The study took three years of full-time work to complete. You are likely to be working with much more restricted time-scales and once again we would emphasise keeping your study small-scale and manageable. The example we are going to work through below has a five-week base-line phase, a 22-week intervention phase; it begins at the start of the Autumn term and ends at the end of the Spring term. It analyses four social behaviours: looking at/towards face; joint focus; social physical contact; and engagement. Five minutes (300 seconds) of video is collected on a weekly basis.

The aim of the data coding is to measure the number of seconds (out of a maximum of 300) that the social behaviour occurs. If your video camera has a timer facility then you will have the option to run a second clock on the screen while you observe. In this example we are going to focus on looking at/towards face. You will need paper and pencil. Play the video tape and let the second counter run on the screen. Every time your pupil looks at or towards the face of the interactive partner note the time and write it down; when your pupil looks away note the time and write it down. Continue doing this for each and every occurrence of looking at/towards the face until the 300 seconds are completed. You may end up with a score sheet like this.

Looking at/towards the face of interactive partner

looking starts	looking stops
27	33
1′ 06	1′ 15
2′ 13	2′ 16
2′ 45	2′ 58
4′ 17	4′ 36

One of the drawbacks of having to look for the timing on the screen is that it can distract your eyes away from the behaviour you are coding and you may momen-tarily miss something. An alternative strategy is to use an audio timing device so that your eyes can remain fixed on the interaction. This can be simply constructed using an audio recording machine and a means of marking second time intervals exactly (a musical metronome is ideal). Using the metronome as your marker, count aloud 1 to 300 seconds into the audio recording machine. Once this is recorded it can be replayed every time you code behaviour. Start the tape and the video recording at exactly the same time and you will be able to hear the exact second of the start and finish of the behaviour.

Looking at/towards the face of interactive partner

looking starts	looking stops
27	33
66	75
133	136
165	178
257	276

We have used both ways successfully and the choice is a matter of individual preference. There are also much more sophisticated ways of doing this using computer software, but this is unnecessary in small-scale studies.

You then need to calculate the total number of seconds for this type of social behaviour. Remember that the seconds will be inclusive, e.g. the third occurrence started at 2 minutes: 13 seconds and stopped at 2 minutes: 16 seconds, therefore the inclusive total is 4 seconds. In the example given here the total number of seconds of looking at/towards face is 55 seconds. This is out of a possible 300 seconds. The percentage incidence can then be calculated as

$$\frac{55}{300} \times \frac{100}{1} = 18.3 \text{ per cent}$$

If you were to do this once each week then you would have five 'percentage scores' from the baseline phase and 16 from the Intensive Interaction phase (there will not be 22 of these because of interruptions for school holidays and possible illness etc.). Prefix your baseline weeks with a 'b' and the Intensive Interaction weeks with an 'i'. You can create a simple chart with the weeks on the horizontal axis and the percentage incidence on the vertical axis using any software spreadsheet package. Insert a blank row between the baseline and intervention scores on the spreadsheet to ensure that a gap appears on the graph so that these two phases are clearly delineated. All the graphs in the six cases featured in this book were prepared in this way. A demonstration example is illustrated in Figure 16.1. Note the gap between b5 and i6 that separates out the two phases making it easier to analyse. Missing are i8 (probable half-term week), i12 (possible illness of one of the participants), i15 and i16 (Christmas vacation), i19 (possible illness) and i22 (probable half-term). You will need to do the same for the other three coded behaviours.

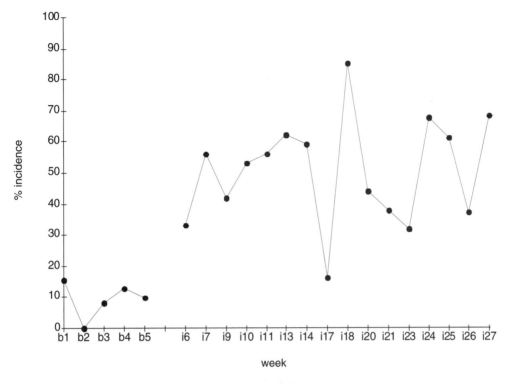

Figure 16.1 Example graph for looking at/towards face

Observation reliability

It is quite probable that some bias may creep into your observation coding. Subconsciously you will want Intensive Interaction to work and you may be over-enthusiastic in your interpretation of behaviours. To strengthen the validity of your study we recommend that about 10 per cent of the data is coded by a person not involved in the research (this is known as 'inter-observer agreement' coding). Work out the number of seconds where coders agree and the number of seconds where coders disagree. An overall inter-observer agreement percentage score can then be calculated by:

$$\frac{\text{number of agreements}}{\text{number of agreements} + \text{disagreements}} \times \frac{100}{1}$$

It is often argued that agreements should be at a minimum level of 80 per cent (Kazdin 1982).

As time progresses you might also find you become a little 'stale' in your behaviour coding and again this might affect the validity of your findings. It is worth re-coding about ten per cent of the data yourself and comparing your two scores to check that levels are not falling below 80 per cent. This is 'intra-observer' agreement coding and it strengthens the validity of your findings.

Triangulation

If you are undertaking a small evaluation project for your own interest, to collect evidence of efficacy or as a means of making small progress steps more visible, then working through the example quoted above should be sufficient for your purposes. If you are undertaking a project of this nature for a larger audience, for public dissemination or for a Masters dissertation, you may need to consider 'triangulating' or 'crystallising' your data with some other measures. The cases featured in this book use two additional standardised measures: the Kiernan and Reid (1987) Pre-Verbal Communication Assessment Schedule and an adaptation of the Brazelton (1984) Cuddliness Scale. The Kiernan and Reid schedule is widely available in schools and frequently used for assessment of pupils with severe and complex learning difficulties. This is a detailed schedule that documents small developmental steps so progress can be easily tracked over time. For a quick 'overview' you can compare overall percentage scores from the schedule by calculating:

$$\frac{\text{number of communication descriptors achieved}}{\text{total number in the schedule}} \times \frac{100}{1}$$

to give a percentage score that can be compared at different time intervals. The adapted Brazelton scale measures readiness for social physical communication and is another useful assessment tool for triangulating your data. It was used with all the pupils featured in this book and is reproduced in Box 16.2. Decide which of the eight statements in Box 16.2 best describes your pupil and note this at the start of the baseline phase. Do the same again at the end of the baseline phase to check whether there has been any progress before Intensive Interaction starts and then at the end of your evaluation study. A useful additional 'probe' point to take is five weeks into the intervention phase, as this is the same length of time as the baseline phase and will show if there is any early progress.

Analysing the data

Analysing your data is a process of scrutinising the data for differing levels of incidence and of detecting patterns. This is more easily done when the data is represented in graph form. For instance you may notice that the baseline phase is relatively flat or that there are early surges in some behaviours which level off. You may notice progress tailing off at the end of terms or that some behaviours develop more quickly than others. It is useful to keep a diary or 'historical log'

1. **Actively** resists being held (e.g. stiffens, thrashes, pushes away)

2. Resists being held **most** but **not all** of the time

3. Does not resist being held but **does not participate** (lies passively)

4. Will **eventually** relax and mould into being held but only after a lot of encouragement

5. Will **usually** relax and mould when **first** held

6. **Always** relaxes and moulds when **first** held

7. Relaxes, moulds and **actively turns head towards** interactive partner

8. **All of above plus** initiates physical contact such as clinging or grasping

Figure 16.2 Physical Sociability Assessment Scale (adapted from Nind 1993 and Brazelton 1984)

during the lifetime of the project in which to record any significant events at home or at school that may affect progress so that these can be analysed alongside the data.

Dissemination

This is a very important part of the research process and can be implemented at many levels. It is vital for the healthy growth of Intensive Interaction that we share our knowledge and experience. At the simplest level you may want to feed back your findings to colleagues in a staff meeting or training event. You may also want to summarise your findings for parents and other interested parties or pin a copy to the staffroom notice board. As we noted in Chapter 13 it is very useful to have written evidence of this kind of evaluation study for Ofsted inspectors. A written report can also form the basis for discussion at a staff appraisal and demonstrate to line managers your interest in wider educational issues. If you are doing an evaluation study as part of a Best Practice project or assignment for a qualification, you will need to check closely with your supervisor about the writing up process. We would like to encourage more practitioners at grass roots level to publish their work and reiterate how much we value these contributions. If you are considering trying to get your work published in a journal then the following tips might be helpful:

- Find out where your nearest higher education institution is and check out the library facilities.
- Ask for assistance – librarians are enormously helpful and resourceful individuals.

- Study the journal catalogue for titles in the inclusive and special education fields; titles that relate to language and communication could also be relevant.
- Read a few articles from journals that you think might be likely targets and get a feel for the kind of work that is featured.
- Scrutinise the conditions set out for article submissions (usually located on the inside cover of the journal) paying particular attention to word length, comments about style, audience and document formatting.
- Note the name and address of the editing person to whom submissions are to be sent.
- Write up your study in the style and formatting recommended by the journal.
- Be careful to reference any cited work and to include a full set of references at the end of your article (formatted according to the journal specifications).
- Get a colleague – or an HE supervisor if you can access one – to look over your article and comment.
- Send off your article with a short, covering letter (only submit to one journal at a time).
- Wait patiently – it might take up to six months to get a reply because editors send submitted articles out to be reviewed by specialists in your field.
- Do not be disheartened if you get a rejection. Take the feedback on board, amend your article, target another journal and have another go.
- Do not be disheartened if you receive a 'provisional' acceptance and you have to make several revisions to satisfy reviewers. This is normal procedure and almost everyone has a few amendments to make.

Some of the journals that have already featured articles about Intensive Interaction include:

- *European Journal of Special Needs Education*
- *International Journal of Disability, Development and Education*
- *British Journal of Special Education*
- *British Journal of Learning Disabilities*
- *Journal of Research in Special Educational Needs*
- *Support for Learning*
- *Child Language, Teaching and Therapy*
- *Children and Society*
- *British Journal of Music Therapy*

Other good sources of dissemination to target are newspapers such as the *TES* or the *Guardian* and teaching magazines such as those in the Scholastic range which are always to be found well thumbed and coffee-stained in school staffrooms. Your findings can also be disseminated through LEA networks and specialist web sites such as the one for Intensive Interaction (www.IntensiveInteraction.co.uk).

CHAPTER 17

Intensive Interaction as the Focus for 'Action Research'

> We are often seeking not simply to understand something, but also to try to change it. Effectively many real world studies are evaluations. They try to provide information about how some intervention, procedure, system, or whatever, is functioning; and how it might be improved. This kind of involved, 'action' agenda brings to the fore many different practical and ethical issues.
>
> (Robson 2002: xvi)

A few efficacy evaluation studies of Intensive Interaction have been undertaken, but even fewer studies have addressed implementation and management elements and you may wish to consider a research project in one of these areas. This kind of research is nearer to the 'critical education' paradigm described in Chapter 15 and is ideally suited to 'action research'.

What is action research?

According to Winter and Munn-Giddings (2001: 8) action research is 'the study of a social situation carried out by those involved in that situation in order to improve both their practice and the quality of their understanding'. It involves planning action on the basis of reflection, observing systematically the process of the planned action, evaluating it and using evidence from the evaluation to inform further planning and action in a spiral of self-reflection. Since reflection is a very important part of Intensive Interaction it would seem a particularly appropriate method to adopt. This does not imply that action research is superior to other methods of research or that it should be considered exclusively. There are many other genres that can also be considered for researching Intensive Interaction. We cannot cover every possibility in this book so we refer you to some excellent methodology text books for further reading:

- Colin Robson (2002) *Real World Research* (2nd edition). Oxford: Blackwell.
- Louis Cohen, Lawrence Manion and Keith Morrison (2000) *Research Methods in Education* (5th edition). London: Routledge.
- Peter Clough and Cathy Nutbrown (2002) *A Student Guide to Methodology*. London: Sage.

Action research has grown in popularity and status in recent years and does not invite the same degree of scepticism from critics who once regarded it as 'soft research'. It is applicable to almost any setting where people and procedures are involved and where change might bring about desirable improvement. It can be undertaken by individual practitioners, groups of practitioners working together, education managers or coordinators and is frequently linked with professional development. A key element in this is empowerment – gaining more professional autonomy through professional development.

Cohen *et al.* (2000: 226 – see above) list some examples of action research in education contexts:

- *teaching methods* – replacing a traditional method by a discovery method;
- *learning strategies* – adopting an integrated approach to learning in preference to a single-subject style of teaching and learning;
- *evaluative procedures* – improving one's methods of continuous assessment;
- *attitudes and values* – encouraging more positive attitudes to work, or modifying pupils' value systems with regard to some aspect of life;
- *continuing professional development of teachers* – improving teaching skills, developing new methods of learning. Increasing powers of analysis, of heightening self-awareness;
- *management and control* – the gradual introduction of the techniques of behaviour modification;
- *administration* – increasing the efficiency of some aspect of the administrative side of school life.

Getting started

Sometimes one of the most difficult aspects of research is getting started. It is not always easy to crystallise our area of interest into a focused research question. Clough and Nutbrown (2002) advocate two strategies that are particularly helpful with this process. The first uses an image of the Russian doll, whereby an original statement is gradually broken down and layers of complexity stripped away until the heart of the question is exposed. The second is their 'Goldilocks' approach – a way of thinking through how a research question is suited to its purpose for that particular researcher, in that particular setting at that particular time. Is it too big (too unwieldy for one researcher)? too small (not enough substance)? too 'hot' (politically or professionally)? too 'cold' (over-researched, stale or old)? etc. until the researcher finds a question that is 'just right' for the particular situation.

If your research project is related to improving practice in your school it is a good idea to set up an initial meeting of all interested parties to discuss ideas and explore initiatives. You may find it helpful to use one or both of Clough and Nutbrown's Goldilocks and Russian doll principles in the discussions.

Cyclical action research process

In Box 17.1 we have set out an example of how the action research process might unfold. It illustrates the kind of action cycle you might typically work through based on the example of a coordinator wanting to research how best to improve record keeping for Intensive Interaction in her/his school.

Some ideas for action research projects

Set out below are some topic areas/ideas that you might want to consider working up into an action research project.

- Intensive Interaction and its impact on teamwork;
- Intensive Interaction and practitioners' emotional well-being;
- using the Audit Framework to enhance Intensive Interaction practice;
- creating better understanding and practice in the reflection and discussion elements of Intensive Interaction;
- planning and recording progress;
- Intensive Interaction and the National Curriculum;
- Intensive Interaction and the impact on children's interactions at home;
- Intensive Interaction and parent involvement;
- enabling peers/friends/siblings to become interactive partners;
- ongoing staff development/Intensive Interaction workshops.

Some final checkpoints

If you are undertaking a research project as part of a qualification, are funded by an external body or are acting in partnership with an organisation external to your school (e.g. an HEI research department) then this creates an additional dimension for potential dissemination. There are other ethical issues to consider and increased levels of access to negotiate.

- Check whether you need permission from your LEA to undertake your proposed study.

Step 1 Defining the enquiry

Reflection: Issue of concern – How can we improve our Intensive Interaction record keeping? Who will be involved – coordinator, head teacher, staff currently practising Intensive Interaction, other interested staff?

Time scale – Spring term

Action: Write a draft proposal setting out the aims of the project, people involved and time scales.

Step 2 What do we need to find out?

Reflection: Why do we feel it is important to keep records? What are they for? Who benefits? What recording is currently happening? How often? By whom? In what form?
What do staff feel about the way Intensive Interaction is currently recorded – A non-event? Inadequate? Helpful? Useful? Useless? Too idiosyncratic? Onerous? Is there anything missing? How effective is it? Is it used and referred to? How often? Does it inform practice? Is it easily processed and accessed? What are the difficulties?

Action: Examine current record systems, policies etc; look at examples of other record-keeping systems from other schools and from literature; talk to staff individually and as a group; design a questionnaire for staff.

Step 3 Data collection and analysis

Reflection: How might I most effectively gather the data I need?

Action: Data collection – make detailed notes of (or tape) individual and group discussions and interviews; administer the questionnaire.
Analysis – synthesise the completed questionnaires, interview notes and observation notes.

Step 4 First review stage

Reflection: Review and reflect on the data.

Action: Identify an issue from the data to address (e.g. feedback showed that many staff felt the reporting system was too ad hoc and when a pupil moved from one class to another continuity was compromised).

Step 5 Implement a change

Reflection: Together with colleagues decide to implement a change based on the issue you identified in step 4 (e.g. design a common recording system to be adopted by all members of staff).

Action: Implement and monitor the change; systematically continue to observe and talk to staff to assess the response to the new system. What do staff find most/least helpful about it? Write down your findings and analyse them in the same way as step 3.

Step 6 Second review stage

Reflection: Review the change – was it worth doing? What were the benefits and the drawbacks? Should we continue with it? Should we abandon it and try something else? Should we expand it? What else should we do (e.g. do we need to look at any other examples of Intensive Interaction record keeping – from other organisations, from the literature)?

Box 17.1 Example of cyclic process in an action research project

---

Action: Decide on a course of action and if this involves introducing further change then go back through the cycle from steps 4 to 6 to monitor this and any subsequent change. Continue this process until you reach a stage where you are satisfied you have resolved your initial issue of concern as set out in step 1.

Step 7 Dissemination

This is an important part of the action research and one that is frequently neglected. Once a change has been worked through and reviewed it is tempting to omit the stage of writing about and sharing it, especially if the change has resulted in improved practice. However, even if you are not doing this project as part of a professional development course or qualification, your findings might be useful to a number of people including your own colleagues and senior managers, other schools in the area, Intensive Interaction practitioners elsewhere, the Intensive Interaction web site (www.IntensiveInteraction.co.uk) and academics. Consider writing up your findings for a journal article (see advice on this above).
The report you prepare should include:
• an explanation of the nature of the enquiry and what you were trying to find out
• a critical appraisal of other studies and literature in this field of enquiry
• an explanation of the methods used to find out your information
• a summary of the relevant information (your data)
• an analysis of this data.

Box 17.1 (continued)

• Be open and honest about the purpose of your study so that no element of deception is involved.
• Be open and honest about any sources of funding so that people can judge whether there is likely to be any conflict of interest or policy-driven bias.
• Decide how terms of anonymity and confidentiality will apply to your study.
• Inform all participants how the information you collect will be used.

Concluding thoughts

We have enjoyed writing this book. It has given us the opportunity to reflect at length on where we have come to with Intensive Interaction, where we are going and what implementation issues we must address if the approach is to continue to evolve. We deliberately chose to base the book around six case studies because Intensive Interaction is about people. It is about interacting and 'being with' individuals who find social communication difficult. In part this book is a celebration of the achievements of those children and the staff who worked with them.

We opted to situate this core element of the case studies within an overall theoretical and discursive framework, so that we could reflect on issues that are important for optimum implementation and continued good practice. In doing so we also addressed wider issues of the school context such as curriculum and inclusion because we need to be continually proactive about Intensive Interaction in terms of policy as well as practice. On another level we attempted to make the research process more transparent and accessible to practitioners and emphasised the important contribution they can make to the body of knowledge on Intensive Interaction. We hope the book will generate more research projects of all different kinds and sizes and that readers will want to be part of an active Intensive Interaction research community that is driven by the two interrelated aims of developing and sharing understanding and improving practice.

References

Ainscow, M. (1999) *Understanding the Development of Inclusive Schools.* London: Falmer.

Ainscow, M. (2000) 'Profile', in Clough. P. and Corbett, J. (eds) *Theories of Inclusive Education: A Students' Guide.* London: Paul Chapman.

Aird, R. (2001) *The Education and Care of Children with Severe, Profound and Multiple Learning Difficulties.* London: David Fulton Publishers.

Allan, J. (2000) 'Reflection: inconclusive education? Towards settled uncertainty', in Clough, P. and Corbett, J. (eds) *Theories of Inclusive Education: A Students' Guide.* London: Paul Chapman.

Alliance for Inclusive Education (2002) www.allfie.org.uk/pages/principles, accessed 27 January 2003.

Babbage, R., Byers, R. and Redding, H. (1999) *Approaches to Teaching and Learning: Including Pupils with Learning Difficulties.* London: David Fulton Publishers.

Ballard, K. (1995) 'Inclusion, paradigms, power and participation', in Clark, C., Dyson, A. and Millward, A. (eds) *Towards Inclusive Schools?* London: David Fulton Publishers.

Barber, M. and Goldbart, J. (1998) 'Accounting for learning and failure to learn in people with profound and multiple learning difficulties', in Lacey, P. and Ouvry, C. (eds) *People with Profound and Multiple Learning Difficulties: A Collaborative Approach to Meeting Complex Needs.* London: David Fulton Publishers.

Barton, L. (1995) 'The politics of education for all', *Support for Learning,* **10** (4), 156–60.

Bateson, M. (1975) 'Mother–infant exchanges: the epigenesis of conversational interaction', in Aaronson, D. and Rieber, R. (eds) *Developmental Psycholinguistics and Communication Disorders.* New York: New York Academy of Sciences.

Bell, R.Q. (1968) 'A reinterpretation of the direction of effects in studies of socialization', *Psychological Review,* 75, 81–95.

Benjamin, S., Nind, M., Sheehy, K., Collins, J. and Hall, K. (2002) 'Moments of inclusion and exclusion: pupils negotiating classroom contexts', paper presented at BERA Annual Conference, University of Exeter, 12–14 September 2002.

Billinge, R. (1987) 'The objectives model of curriculum development – a creaking bandwagon', *Mental Handicap*, **16**, 26–9.

Blenkin, G.M. (1994) 'Early learning and a developmentally appropriate curriculum: some lessons from research', in Blenkin, G.M. and Kelly, A.V. (eds) *The National Curriculum and Early Learning: An Evaluation*. London: Paul Chapman.

Blenkin, G.M. and Kelly, A.V. (1993) 'Never mind the quality feel the breadth and balance', in Campbell, R.J. (ed.) *Breadth and Balance in the Primary Curriculum*. London: Falmer Press.

Booth, T. (1992) *Learning for All: Unit 1/2 Making Connections*. Bristol: The Open University.

Booth, T., Ainscow, M., Black-Hawkins, K., Vaughan, M. and Shaw, L. (2000) *Index for Inclusion: developing learning and participation in schools*. Bristol: CSIE.

Brazelton, T.B. (1979) 'Evidence of communication during neonatal behavioural assessment', in Bullowa, M. (ed.) *Before Speech*. Cambridge: Cambridge University Press.

Brazelton, T.B. (1984) *Neonatal Behaviour Assessment Scale*. London: Heinemann Medical Books.

Brazelton, T.B., Koslowski, B. and Main, M. (1974) 'The origins of reciprocity: The early mother–infant interaction', in Lewis, M. and Rosenblum, L.A. (eds) *The Effect of the Infant on its Caregiver*. New York: Wiley.

Bretherton, I., Bates, E., Benigni, L., Camaioni, L. and Volterra, V. (1979) 'Relationships between cognition, communication and quality of attachment', in Bates, E. (ed.) *The Emergence of Symbols: Cognition and Communication in Infancy*. New York: Academic Press.

Bromwich, R.M. (1981) *Working with Parents and Infants: An Interactional Approach*. Baltimore: University Press.

Bruner, J. (1975) 'The ontogenesis of speech acts', *Journal of Child Language*, **2**, 1–19.

Bullowa, M. (ed.) (1979) *Before Speech*. Cambridge: Cambridge University Press.

Byers, R. (1994) 'Teaching as dialogue: Teaching approaches and learning styles in schools for pupils with learning difficulties', in Coupe O'Kane, J. and Smith, B. (eds) *Taking Control: Enabling people with learning difficulties*. London: David Fulton Publishers.

Byers, R. (1999) 'Experience and achievement: initiatives in curriculum development for pupils with severe and profound and multiple learning difficulties', *British Journal of Special Education*, **26**, 184–8.

Byers, R. and Rose, R. (1994) 'Schools should decide . . .', in Rose, R., Fergusson, A., Coles, C., Byers, R. and Banes, D. (eds) *Implementing the Whole Curriculum for Pupils with Learning Difficulties*. London: David Fulton Publishers.

Byers, R., Dee, L., Hayhoe, H. and Maudsley, L. (2002) *Enhancing Quality of Life: Facilitating transitions for people with profound and complex learning difficulties.* London: Skill/University of Cambridge.

Caldwell, P. (2002) *Learning the Language: Building Relationships with People with Severe Learning Disability, Autistic Spectrum Disorder and Other Challenging Behaviours.* Brighton: Pavilion.

Calhoun, M.L. and Rose, T.L. (1988) 'The early social reciprocity intervention for infants with severe retardation: Current findings and implications for the future', *Education and Training in Mental Retardation*, **23** (4), 340–3.

Carlson, L. and Bricker, D.D. (1982) 'Dyadic and contingent aspects of early communicative intervention', in Bricker. D.D. (ed.) *Interventions with At Risk and Handicapped Infants.* Baltimore: University Park Press.

Carpenter, B., Ashdown, R. and Bovair, K. (1996) *Enabling Access: Effective Teaching and Learning for Pupils with Learning Difficulties.* London: David Fulton Publishers.

Cheung, M.Y.M. (1999) 'The process of innovation adoption and teacher development', *Education and Research in Education*, **13** (2), 55–75.

Clark, G.N. and Seifer, R. (1983) 'Facilitating mother–infant communication: a treatment model for high-risk and developmentally delayed infants', *Infant Mental Health Journal*, **4** (2), 67–82.

Clough, P. (2000) 'Routes to inclusion', in Clough. P. and Corbett, J. (eds) *Theories of Inclusive Education: A Students' Guide.* London: Paul Chapman.

Clough, P. and Nutbrown, C. (2002) *A Student Guide to Methodology.* London: Sage.

Cohen, L., Manion, L. and Morrison, K. (2000) *Research Methods in Education* (5th edition). London: Routledge.

Cohen, M. (1988) 'Designing state assessment systems', *Phi Delta Kappau*, **70** (8), 593–8.

Cole, A. and Lloyd, A. (2002) 'It's not what you know it's who! Enabling and supporting community involvement', in Carnaby, S. (ed.) *Learning Disability Today.* Brighton: Pavilion/Foundation for People with Learning Disabilities/Tizard Centre.

Collins, J., Harkin, J. and Nind, M. (2002) *Manifesto for Learning.* London: Continuum.

Collis, M. and Lacey, P. (1996) *Interactive Approaches to Teaching.* London: David Fulton Publishers.

Corbett, J. (1997) 'Include/exclude: redefining the boundaries', *International Journal of Inclusive Education*, **1**(1), 55–64.

Corbett, J. (1999) 'Inclusive education and school culture', *International Journal of Inclusive Education*, **3** (1), 53–61.

Corbett, J. (2001) 'Teaching approaches which support inclusive education: a connective pedagogy', *British Journal of Special Education*, **28** (2), 55–9.

Cornell, B. and Garden, N. (1990) 'Principles must come first', *British Journal of Special Education*, **17** (1), 4–7.

Crawford, A.R. (1997) 'Professional development: Supporting instructional change through teacher reflection', *The Professional Educator*, **19** (2), 1–11.

Crawford, J., Brockel, B., Schauss, S. and Miltenberger, R.G. (1992) 'A comparison of methods for the functional assessment of stereotypic behavior', *JASH*, **17** (2), 77–86.

Cuban, L. (1988) 'A fundamental puzzle of school reform', *Phi Delta Kappau*, **70** (5), 341–4.

Culham, A. and Nind, M. (in press) 'A critical analysis of normalisation: clearing the way for inclusion', *Journal of Intellectual and Developmental Disability*.

Davies, G. (1997) 'Communication', in Powell. S. and Jordan, R. (eds) *Autism and Learning: a Guide to Good Practice*. London: David Fulton Publishers.

Davis, J. (2001) *A Sensory Approach to the Curriculum for Pupils with Profound and Multiple Learning Difficulties*. London: David Fulton Publishers.

Dawson, G. and Osterling, J. (1997) 'Early intervention in autism', in Guralnick, M. (ed.) *The Effectiveness of Early Intervention*. Baltimore MD: Brookes.

DfES (2001) *Special Educational Needs Code of Practice*. London: DfES.

Dunst, C.J. and Trivette, C.M. (1986) 'Looking beyond the parent–infant dyad for the determinants of maternal styles of interaction', *Infant Mental Health Journal*, **7**, 69–80.

Ephraim, G.W.E. (1979) Developmental Process in Mental Handicap: A Generative Structure Approach. Unpublished PhD thesis, Brunel University, Uxbridge.

Ephraim, G. (1989) 'Idiosyncratic behaviour and how to encourage it!' *Talking Sense*, Summer, 12–15.

Field, T.M. (1978) 'The three R's of infant–adult interactions: Rhythms, repertoires and responsivity', *Journal of Paediatric Psychology*, **3** (3), 131–6.

Field, T.M. (1979) 'Games parents play with normal and high risk infants', *Child Psychology and Human Development*, **10** (1), 41–8.

Fisher, A. (1994) An investigation of two contrasting teaching approaches with a group of profound and multiply impaired pupils. Unpublished M.Ed thesis, Heriot-Watt University, Edinburgh.

Fogel, A. (1977) 'Temporal organisation in mother–infant face-to-face interaction', in Schaffer, H.R. (ed.) *Studies in Mother–Infant Interaction*. London: Academic Press.

Fraiberg, S. (1974) 'Blind infants and their mothers: an examination of the sign system', in Lewis, M. and Rosenblum, L.A. (eds) *The Effect of the Infant on its Caregiver*. London: John Wiley.

Fullan, M. (1991) *The New Meaning of Educational Change*, 2nd edition. London: Cassell.

Fuller, F. I. (1969) 'Concerns of teachers', *American Educational Research Journal*, **6**, 207–26.

Garner, P., Hinchcliffe, V. and Sandow, S. (1995) *What Teachers Do: Developments in Special Education*. London: Chapman.

Georgiades, N.J. and Phillimore, L. (1980) 'The myth of the hero-innovator', in Kiernan, C.C. and Wood, P.F. (eds) *Behaviour Modification with the Severely Retarded*. Amsterdam: Associated Scientific Publishers.

Gersten, R. (1996) 'Literacy instruction for language-minority students: The transition years', *Elementary School Journal*, **96**, 227–44.

Gersten, R., Baker, S. and Lloyd, J.W. (2000) 'Designing high quality research in special education: group experimental design', *Journal of Special Education*, **34** (1), 2–29.

Gillman, M., Swain, J. and Heyman, B. (1997) 'Life history of "case" history: the objectification of people with learning difficulties through the tyranny of professional discourses', *Disability and Society*, **12** (5), 675–93.

Goldberg, S. (1977) 'Social competence in infancy: a model of parent–infant interaction', *Merrill-Palmer Quarterly*, **23**, 163–77.

Grove, N. and Peacey, N. (1999) 'Teaching subjects to pupils with profound and multiple learning difficulties: considerations for the new framework', *British Journal of Special Education*, **26** (2), 83–6.

Hall, G.E. (1979) 'The concerns-based approach for facilitating change', *Educational Horizons*, **57**, 202–8.

Hall, G.E. and Hord, S.M. (1987) *Change in Schools: Facilitating the Process*. Albany: SUNY Press.

Hall, G.E., George, A.A. and Rutherford, W.L. (1986) *Measuring Stages of Concern about the Innovation: A Manual for the Use of the SoC Questionnaire*. Austin: Research and Development Centre for Teacher Education, University of Texas.

Hannan, A., English, S. and Silver, H. (1999) 'Why innovate? Some preliminary findings from a research based project on innovations in teaching and learning', *Studies in Higher Education*, **24** (3), 279–89.

Harding, C. (1983) 'Setting the stage for language acquisition: communication development in the first year', in Golinkoff, R. (ed.) *The Transition from Pre-Linguistic to Linguistic Communication*. New Jersey: Lawrence Erlbaum Associates.

Hart, S. (in press) 'Learning without limits', in Nind, M., Sheehy, K. and Simmons, K. (eds) *Inclusive Education: Diverse Learners and Learning Contexts*. London: David Fulton Publishers. (provisional title)

Hewett, D. (1995) Understanding and Writing a Methodology of Intensive Interaction – Teaching Pre-Speech Communication Abilities to Learners with Severe Learning Difficulties: A Naturalistic Inquiry Using Qualitative Evaluation Methods. Unpublished PhD Thesis, Cambridge Institute of Education.

Hewett, D. and Nind, M. (eds) (1998) *Interaction in Action: Reflections on the Use of Intensive Interaction*. London: David Fulton Publishers.

Hord, S.M., Rutherford, W.L., Huling-Austin, L. and Hall, G.E. (1987) *Taking Charge of Change*. Alexandria: Association for Supervision and Curriculum Development.

Hoyle, E. (1986) *The Politics of School Management*. London: Hodder and Stoughton.

Huberman, M. (1981) *Exemplary Center for Reading Instruction (ECRI), Maespa, North Plains: a case study*. Andover, MA: The Network.

Huberman, M. and Miles, M. (1984) *Innovation Up Close*. New York: Penguin.

Hughes, M. and Westgate, D. (1997) 'Assistants as talk partners in early-years classrooms', *Educational Review*, **49**, 5–12.

Irvine, C. (1998) 'Addressing the needs of adults with profound and multiple learning disabilities in social services provision', in Hewett, D. and Nind, M. (eds) *Interaction in Action: Reflections on the Use of Intensive Interaction*. London: David Fulton Publishers.

Jackson, M. (2000) 'Introduction', in Brigham, L., Atkinson, D., Jackson, M., Rolph, S. and Walmsley, J. (eds) *Crossing Boundaries: Change and Continuity in the History of Learning Disability*. Kidderminster: BILD Publications.

Jackson, S. and Martin, P.Y. (1998) 'Surviving the care system: education and resilience', *Journal of Adolescence*, **21**, 569–83.

Joyce, B. and Showers, B. (1988) *Student Achievement Through Staff Development*. New York: Longman.

Kaufman, B.N. (1994) *Son Rise: The Miracle Continues*. Tiburon, CA: H.J. Kramer Inc.

Kaye, K. and Fogel, A. (1980) 'The temporal structure of face-to-face communication between mothers and infants', *Developmental Psychology*, **5**, 454–64.

Kazdin, A.E. (1982) *Single Case Research Designs: Methods for Clinical and Applied Settings*. Oxford: Oxford University Press.

Kellett, M. (2000) 'Sam's story: evaluating Intensive Interaction in terms of its effect on the social and communicative ability of a young child with severe learning difficulties', *Support for Learning*, **15** (4), 165–71.

Kellett, M. (2001) Implementing Intensive Interaction: an evaluation of the efficacy of Intensive Interaction in promoting sociability and communication in young children who have severe learning difficulties and of factors affecting its implementation in community special schools. Unpublished PhD Thesis, Oxford Brookes University.

Kellett, M. (2003) 'Jacob's Journey: developing sociability and communication in a young boy with severe and complex learning difficulties using the Intensive Interaction teaching approach', *Journal of Research in Special Educational Needs*, March.

Kellett M. and Nind, M. (2001) 'Ethics in quasi-experimental research "on" people with severe learning disabilities: dilemmas and compromises', *British Journal of Learning Disabilities*, **29**, 52–5.

Kelly, V. (1994) 'Beyond the rhetoric and the discourse', in Blenkin, G.M. and Kelly, A.V. (eds) *The National Curriculum and Early Learning: An Evaluation.* London: Paul Chapman.

Kiernan, C. and Reid, B. (1987) *Pre-Verbal Communication Schedule.* Windsor: NFER-Nelson.

Kinder, K., Wakefield, A. and Wilkin, A. (1996) *Talking Back: Pupils' Views on Disaffection.* Slough: NFER.

Klinger, L.G. and Dawson, G. (1992) 'Facilitating early social development in children with autism', in Warren, S.F. and Reichle, J. (eds) *Causes and Effects in Communication and Language.* Baltimore, MD and London: Paul Brookes.

Knight, C. and Watson, J. (1990) *Intensive Interactive Teaching at Gogarburn School.* Moray House College publication.

Knott, L. (1998) 'Ben's Story: Developing the communication abilities of a pupil with autism', in Hewett, D. and Nind, M. (eds) *Interaction in Action: Reflections on the Use of Intensive Interaction*, London: David Fulton Publishers.

Langley, M.B. and Lombardino, L.J. (1987) 'Application of a normal developmental model for understanding the communicative behaviours of students with severe handicaps', *European Journal of Special Needs in Education*, **2** (3), 161–75.

Lester, N.B. and Onore, C.S. (1990) *Learning Change: One school district meets language across the curriculum.* Portsmouth, NH: Boynton Cook.

Liberman, A. (ed.) (1995) *The Work of Restructuring Schools: Building from the ground up.* New York: Teachers College Press.

Linfoot, K. (1994) 'Communicative behaviour in the least restrictive environment', in Linfoot, K. (ed.) *Communication Strategies for People with Developmental Disabilities.* Atarmon, Australia: MacLennan and Petty Ltd.

Lipsky, D.K. and Gartner, A. (1999) 'Inclusive education: a requirement of a democratic society', in Daniels, H. and Garner, P. (eds) *Inclusive Education: Supporting Inclusion in Education Systems.* London: Kogan Page.

Lloyd, C. (1997) 'Inclusive education for children with special educational needs in the early years', in Wolfendale, S. (ed.) *Meeting Special Needs in the Early Years: Directions in Policy and Practice.* London: David Fulton Publishers.

Lock, A. (1978) *Action, Gesture and Symbol.* London: Academic Press.

Macdonald, B. (1974) *SAFARI – an abstract of the proposal submitted to the Ford Foundation in 1971, SAFARI Innovation, Evaluation, Research and the Problem of Control.* Norwich Centre for Applied Research in Education, University of East Anglia.

Mamlin, N. (1999) 'Despite best intentions: When inclusion fails', *Journal of Special Education*, **33** (1), 36–49.

Maskell, S., Watkins, F., Haworth, E. and Brown, E. (2001) *Baseline Assessment, Curriculum and Target Setting for Pupils with Profound and Multiple Learning Difficulties*. London: David Fulton Publishers.

McCollum, J. (1984) 'Social interaction between parents and babies: validation of an intervention procedure', *Child Care, Health and Development*, **10**, 301–15.

McConkey, R. (1981) 'Education without understanding', *Special Education: Forward Trends*, **8** (3), 8–11.

McKinney, M., Sexton, T. and Meyerson, M.J. (1999) 'Validating the efficacy-based change model', *Teaching and Teacher Education*, **115**, 471–85.

Mittler, P. (2000a) *Working Towards Inclusive Education: Social Contexts*. London: David Fulton Publishers.

Mittler, P. (2000b) 'Profile', in Clough, P. and Corbett, J. (eds) *Theories of Inclusive Education: A Students' Guide*. London: Paul Chapman.

Murdoch, H. (1997) 'Stereotyped behaviours: how should we think about them?' *British Journal of Special Education*, **24** (2), 71–5.

Nadel, J. and Camaioni, L. (1993) (eds) *New Perspectives in Early Communicative Development*. London and New York: Routledge.

NCC (1990) *Curriculum Guidance 3: The Whole Curriculum*. York: NCC.

Newson, J. (1979) 'Intentional behaviour in the young infant', in Shaffer, D. and Dunn, J. (eds) *The First Year of Life*. New York: Wiley.

Nind, M. (1993) Access to Communication: Efficacy of Intensive Interaction teaching for people with severe developmental disabilities who demonstrate ritualistic behaviours. Unpublished PhD thesis, Cambridge Institute of Education.

Nind, M. (1996) 'Efficacy of Intensive Interaction: Developing sociability and communication in people with severe and complex learning difficulties using an approach based on caregiver–infant interaction', *European Journal of Special Educational Needs*, **11** (1), 48–66.

Nind, M. (1999) 'Intensive Interaction and autism: A useful approach?' *British Journal of Special Education*, **26** (2), 96–102.

Nind, M. (2000) 'Teachers' understanding of interactive approaches in special education', *International Journal of Disability and Education*, **47** (2), 183–99.

Nind, M. (2001) 'Stereotyped behaviour: resistance by people with profound learning difficulties?' Paper presented at Testimonies of Resistance in Learning Disability History, The Open University, 5 December 2001.

Nind, M. (2002) 'Early childhood education and special needs education: some neglected common ground?' *Westminster Studies in Education*, **25** (1), 77–90.

Nind, M. and Cochrane, S. (2002) 'Inclusive curricula? Pupils on the margins of special schools', *International Journal of Inclusive Education*, **6** (2), 185–98.

Nind, M. and Hewett, D. (1994) *Access to Communication: Developing the Basics of Communication in People with Severe Learning Difficulties Through Intensive Interaction*. London: David Fulton Publishers.

Nind, M. and Hewett, D. (2001) *A Practical Guide to Intensive Interaction.* Kidderminster: BILD Publications.

Nind, M. and Kellett, M. (2002) 'Responding to individuals with severe learning difficulties and stereotyped behaviour: challenges for an inclusive era', *European Journal of Special Needs Education,* **17** (3), 265–82 (and commentaries by Goldbart, J., Harris, J. and Hogg, J., 232–97; and response by Nind and Kellett, 299–300).

Nind, M., Kellett, M. and Hopkins, V. (2001) 'Teachers' talk styles: communication with learners with severe learning difficulties', *Child Language, Teaching and Therapy,* **17** (2), 1–17.

Nind, M. and Powell, S. (2000) 'Intensive Interaction and autism: some theoretical concerns', *Children and Society,* **14** (2), 98–109.

Noad, B. (1995) 'Using a concerns based adoption model to bring about change in adult corrections education', *Australian Journal of Adult and Community Education,* **35** (19), 43–9.

Norwich, B. (1990) 'How an entitlement can become a restraint', in Daniels, H. and Ware, J. (eds) *Special Educational Needs and the National Curriculum.* London: Kogan Page.

Ofsted (1996/1997) *The Annual Report of Her Majesty's Chief Inspector for Schools: Standards and Quality in Education 1996/97.* London: The Stationery Office.

Ofsted (2000) *Writing about Educational Inclusion: Guidance for Inspectors for Writing about Educational Inclusion in Inspection Reports.* www.ofsted.gov.uk/ publications, accessed 29 January 2003.

Ohlhausen, M.M., Meyerson, M.J. and Sexton, T. (1992) 'Viewing innovations through the Efficacy-Based Change Model: A whole language application', *Journal of Reading,* **35**, 536–41.

Ouvry, C. and Saunders, S. (1996) 'Pupils with profound and multiple learning difficulties', in Ashdown, R., Carpenter, B. and Bovair, K. (eds) *Enabling Access: Effective Teaching and Learning for Pupils with Learning Difficulties.* London: David Fulton Publishers.

Papousek, H. and Papousek, M. (1977) 'Mothering and the cognitive head-start', in Schaffer, H.R. (ed.) *Studies in Mother–Infant Interaction.* London: Academic Press.

Pawlby, S.J. (1977) 'Imitative Interaction', in Schaffer, H.R. (ed.) (1977) *Studies in Mother–Infant Interaction.* London: Academic Press.

Pedron, N.A. and Evans, S.B. (1990) 'Modifying classroom teachers' acceptance of the consulting teacher model', *Journal of Educational and Psychological Consultation,* **1** (2), 189–200.

Phillips, C., Chesworth, L., Baker, A. and Jenner, H. (in press) 'Inclusion at Bangabandhu School', in Nind, M., Rix, J., Sheehy, K. and Simmons, K. (eds) *Inclusive Education: Diverse Perspectives.* London: David Fulton Publishers.

Potter, C. and Whittaker, C. (2001) *Enabling Communication in Children with Autism.* London: Jessica Kingsley.

Pugh, G. (1996) (ed.) *Contemporary Issues in the Early Years: Working Collaboratively for Children.* London: Paul Chapman.

QCA (Qualifications and Curriculum Authority) (1999) *Early Learning Goals.* London: QCA/DfEE.

QCA (Qualifications and Curriculum Authority) (2001a) *Planning, teaching and assessing the curriculum for pupils with learning difficulties: General Guidelines.* London: QCA/DfEE.

QCA (Qualifications and Curriculum Authority) (2001b) *Planning, teaching and assessing the curriculum for pupils with learning difficulties: Developing Skills.* London: QCA/DfEE.

Robson, C. (2002) *Real World Research*, 2nd edition. Oxford: Blackwell.

Rogers, E.M. (1995) *Diffusion of Innovation*, 4th edition. London: Macmillan and The Free Press.

Sameroff, A. (1975) 'Transactional models in early social interactions', *Human Development*, **18**, 65–79.

Samuel, J. (2001) 'Intensive Interaction', *Clinical Psychology Forum*, **148**, 22–5.

Samuel, J. and Maggs, J. (1998) 'Introducing Intensive Interaction to people with profound learning difficulties living in small staffed houses in the community', in Hewett, D. and Nind, M. (eds*) Interaction in Action: Reflections on the use of Intensive Interaction.* London: David Fulton Publishers.

Sandberg, A.D., Ehlers, S., Hagberg, B. and Gillberg, C. (2000) 'The Rett Syndrome Complex: Communicative functions in relation to developmental level and autistic features', *Autism*, **4** (3), 249–67.

Sarason, S.B. (1996) *Revisiting 'The Culture of the School and the Problem of Change'.* New York: Teachers College Press.

SCAA (1996) *Assessment, Recording and Accreditation of Achievement for Pupils with Learning Difficulties.* London: DfEE.

SCAA (1997) *Keeping the Curriculum Under Review: Curriculum Planning and Development.* London: SCAA.

Schaffer, H.R. (1977) (ed.) *Studies in Mother–Infant Interaction.* London: Academic Press.

Sebba, J., Byers, R. and Rose, R. (1995) *Redefining the Whole Curriculum for Pupils with Learning Difficulties*, 2nd edition. London: David Fulton Publishers.

Siegel-Causey, E. and Bashinski, S.M. (1997) 'Enhancing initial communication and responsiveness of learners with multiple disabilities: A tri-focus framework for partners', *Focus on Autism and Other Developmental Disabilities*, **12** (2), 105–20.

Siegel-Causey, E. and Wetherby, A. (1993) 'Nonsymbolic communication', in Snell, M.E. (ed.) *Instruction of Students with Severe Learning Disabilities.* New Jersey: Merril.

Slee, R. (1999) 'Policies and practices? Inclusive education and its effects on schooling', in Daniels, H. and Garner, P. (eds) *Inclusive Education.* London: Kogan Page.

Smith, B. (1987) (ed.) *Interactive Approaches to teaching the core subjects.* Bristol: Lame Duck.

Smith, B., Moore, Y. and Phillips, C.J. (1983) 'Education with understanding', *Special Education: Future Trends,* **9** (2), 21–4.

Smith, C. (1998) 'Jamie's story: Intensive Interaction in a College of Further Education', in Hewett, D. and Nind, M. (eds) (1998) *Interaction in Action: Reflections on the Use of Intensive Interaction.* London: David Fulton Publishers.

Somerset Partnership NHS and Social Care Trust (2002) *Intensive Interaction Guidelines.* Somerset Learning Disability Services.

Stern, D. N. (1974) 'Mother and infant at play: the dyadic interaction involving facial, vocal and gaze behaviours', in Lewis, M.and Rosenblum, L.A. (eds) *The Effect of the Infant on its Caregiver.* New York: Wiley.

Stern, D.N. (1977) *The First Relationship.* Cambridge, MA: Harvard University Press.

Stern, D.N. (1985) *The Interpersonal World of the Infant.* New York: Basic Books.

Stothard, V. (1998) 'The gradual development of Intensive Interaction in a school setting', in Hewett, D. and Nind, M. (eds) *Interaction in Action: Reflections on the Use of Intensive Interaction.* London: David Fulton Publishers.

Sylva, K., Siraj-Blatchford, I. and Johnson, S. (1992) 'The impact of the UK National Curriuculum on pre-school practice: some top-down processes at work', *Journal of Early Childhood,* 24 (1), 41–51.

Taylor, B. and Taylor, S. (1998) 'Gary's story: Parents doing Intensive Interaction', in Hewett, D. and Nind, M. (eds) (1998) *Interaction in Action: Reflections on the Use of Intensive Interaction.* London: David Fulton Publishers.

Thomas, G. and Loxley, A. (2001) *Deconstructing Special Education and Constructing Inclusion.* Buckingham: Open University Press.

Thomas, G., Walker, D. and Webb, J. (1998) *The Making of the Inclusive School.* London: Routledge.

Trevarthen, C. (1974) 'Conversations with a two-month-old', *New Scientist,* 230–5.

Trevarthen, C. (1977) 'Emotions in infancy: Regulations of contact and relationships with persons', in Scherer, K.R. and Ekman, P. (eds) *Approaches to Emotion.* New Jersey: Erlbaum Associates.

Trevarthen, C. (1979) 'Communication and cooperation in early infancy: a description of primary intersubjectivity', in Bullowa, M. (ed.) *Before Speech.* Cambridge: Cambridge University Press.

Van den Berg, R. (1993) 'The concerns-based adoption model in the Netherlands, Flanders and the United Kingdom: State of the art and perspective', *Studies in Educational Evaluation,* **19,** 51–63.

Van den Berg, R., Vandenberghe, R. and Sleegers, P. (1999) 'Management of innovations from a cultural-individual perspective', *School of Effectiveness and School Improvement*, **10** (3), 321–51.

Ware, J. (1987) Providing education for children with profound and multiple learning difficulties: A survey of resources and an analysis of staff–pupil interactions in special care units. Unpublished PhD thesis, University of London Institute of Education.

Ware, J. (1994) (ed.) *Educating Children with Profound and Multiple Learning Difficulties.* London: David Fulton Publishers.

Ware, J. (1996) *Creating a Responsive Environment.* London: David Fulton Publishers.

Ware, J. and Healey, I. (1994) 'Conceptualizing progress in children with profound and multiple learning difficulties', in Ware, J. (ed.) *Educating Children with Profound and Multiple Learning Difficulties.* London: David Fulton Publishers.

Watson, J. and Fisher, A. (1997) 'Evaluating the effectiveness of Intensive Interaction teaching with pupils with profound and complex learning difficulties', *British Journal of Special Education*, **24** (2), 80–7.

Watson. J. and Knight, C. (1991) 'An evaluation of intensive interactive teaching with pupils with severe learning difficulties', *Child Language Teaching and Therapy*, **7** (3), 10–25.

Weiner, B. (1986) *An Attribution Theory of Motivation and Emotion.* New York: Springer-Verlag.

Weistuch, L. and Byers-Brown, B. (1987) 'Motherese as therapy: a programme and its dissemination', *Child Language Teaching and Therapy*, **3**, 57–71.

Wenger, E. (1998) *Communities of Practice: Learning, Meaning and Identity.* Cambridge: Cambridge University Press.

Wetherby, A. and Prizant, B.M. (1992) 'Profiling young children's communicative competence', in Warren, S.F. (ed.) *Causes and Effects in Communication and Language.* Baltimore and London: Paul Brookes.

Whalley, M. (1994) *Learning to Be Strong: Setting up a Neighbourhood Service for Under-fives and their Families.* London: Hodder and Stoughton.

Williams, S.R. and Baxter, J.A. (1996) 'Dilemmas of discourse in one middle school mathematics classroom', *Elementary School Journal*, **97**, 21–38.

Winter, R. and Munn-Giddings, C. (2001) *A Handbook for Action Research in Health and Social Care.* London: Routledge.

Wood, S. and Shears, B. (1986) *Teaching Children with Severe Learning Difficulties: A Radical Reappraisal.* London: Croom Helm.

Index

The letter 'b' after a page number indicates a box, or box and text; an 'f' indicates a figure, or figure and text; and a 't' indicates a table, or table and text.